440 - 435 - 8860

Pastor's Pal

William L. Banks

CLC
PUBLICATIONS
Fort Washington, PA 19034

• Pastor's Pal •

Published by CLC ✦ Publications

U.S.A.
P.O. Box 1449, Fort Washington, PA 19034

GREAT BRITAIN
51 The Dean, Alresford, Hants. SO24 9BJ

AUSTRALIA
P.O. Box 2299, Strathpine, QLD 4500

NEW ZEALAND
10 MacArthur Street, Feilding

ISBN 978-0-87508-874-7

Contents

Advice to the New (and Otherwise) Pastor:

FEED MY SHEEP

"*Once there was a young preacher who set out to destroy the goats when the Word of the Lord came to him—Feed My Sheep!*" (S.E. Nothstine, *Moody Monthly*).

I had been in the ministry only a few months when I discovered in the church of which I was the pastor some "strange children." They professed to be saved and sanctified, and yet by their fruits I knew them to be of the same group which the Lord Jesus denounced in Matthew 23. So under the guidance of the Holy Spirit (as I believed), I prepared a message on: "Religious, but Not Christian," using as my text the verse, Matthew 5:20.

That Sunday night I "laid them low." I cut "a wide swath with the gospel sword," "slapped them first on one side and then the other," "gave them both barrels," and "let the chips fall where they would." How I did preach! After the service I went home in high spirits. I had really preached the "rugged gospel." Only once had I been in the brush, so to speak, and then I had cut myself a big stick and clubbed my way out. Yes, I had really had myself a time!

But that night, as I sat alone on the front porch, meditating, I didn't feel quite so elated as I thought I should. As I pondered upon the message I spoke to my Lord. "I sure did preach tonight, didn't I?" Came the answer: "Yes, you surely did." I tried again. "It was scriptural, wasn't it?" No answer. "But Lord, You did it, didn't You? Matthew twenty-three." "Yes, I did do it."

Thinking of nothing more to say, I kept quiet. And so did the Lord. Finally I made ready to retire and had my evening prayer. More silence on the Lord's part. At worship time the next morning I was reading in John, chapter twenty-one, and a question suddenly stood out in letters of fire: "Lovest thou Me?" I stopped reading, and after thinking a bit I said, "Yes, Lord I love You." Silence. And I read on. "Feed My lambs." "But Lord, these are not Your lambs. These are just troublesome old goats!" Silence. I started to read again. But there were the words again in flaming letters: "Feed My sheep."

"But Lord, they are not even sheep! They are goats, driving out many lambs, causing trouble!" Silence. And so I continued to read—and again came that burning question, "Lovest thou Me?" With tear-dimmed eyes I spoke. "Lord, I love You more than anyone or anything in this life or the next, and I want only to do Your will." Still silence! I glanced again at my open New Testament. All I could see was: "Feed My sheep."

"Feed My sheep!" Light began to dawn. And I said, "Lord, I am sorry. I only thought I was doing right about those hypocritical goats." The soft voice seemed to speak directly to me. "Son, I died for all. There are no goats this side of the great judgment." (That was Lesson No. 1.) "And, son, don't worry so much about these 'others.' Just take good care of My sheep. Do not let one go astray. And feed them." (That was Lesson No. 2.)

"And son, if you really feed them, they will grow strong and healthy, and these 'others' will want what My sheep are feeding on. And don't throw rocks and clubs at the 'others' for they will dodge and the stone or club may hit one of My lambs and seriously injure it. No, son, don't throw rocks, but feed My sheep!" (Lesson No. 3.) Did I hear a sob in that voice? Was my Lord weeping?

"Son, feed them. My sheep—feed them. All week long they are stoned and clubbed by the world, and on Sunday they come to My house with heavy loads upon their hearts—and they are hungry. Feed them. Give them something to ease the burden, the loads they are carrying. And feed them—feed them!" (Lesson No. 4.)

Now I was sure there was a catch in that voice. I could not look up. I slid off my chair and buried my face in my hands. And weeping bitter tears of repentance, I asked the Lord to help me remember in the years to come the lessons I learned that morning.

CALLING

According to what is termed the priesthood of all believers, every Christian has the responsibility and right to propagate his or her faith. In this sense all Christians are preachers. However, not all Christians are called to obey the principle established in 1 Corinthians 9:14, which states "those who preach the gospel should live from the gospel." This text teaches the responsibility of the church to maintain the pastor (cf. 1 Tim. 5:17). No man takes this work upon himself. He must be called by God even as Aaron was (Heb. 5:4). And the preacher should know that God called him. Indeed for preachers the call is indispensable.

The Lord Jehovah spoke to Moses from a burning bush. Jeremiah was called. Amos was called. The disciples were called both to discipleship and to special service. And Saul of Tarsus said, "It pleased God, who separated me from my mother's womb and called me through His grace, to reveal His Son in me, that I might preach Him among the Gentiles" (Gal. 1:15–16). Paul was ever grateful to God for "putting him into the ministry" (1 Tim. 1:12). And later, just prior to Paul's first missionary journey, the Holy Spirit said, "Now separate to Me Barnabas and Saul for the work to which I have called them" (Acts 13:2). So the same God who calls into the ministry also sends out. Indeed the Holy Spirit is the One who makes men overseers of churches (Acts 20:28). It is believed that every preacher must have the sincere conviction that the Lord has indeed laid His hand upon him. For preachers—pastors who are also teachers—are God's gifts to His church, men specially chosen by God to function in this special way in the church, the body of Christ. Such is the nature of the work and such is the complexity of the pastor's role that the calling of God is a must. Paul would say a man must have a woe-is-me-if-I-do-not-preach attitude.

Now it may well be that several factors exist which have caused the concept of a calling to be played down or dismissed entirely. There is the desire for a degree issued by that professional school known as a seminary. Education certainly is desirable. But obtaining a seminary degree is not a substitute for a divine calling. The use of degrees has tended to heighten professionalism and obscure the idea of a calling.

In an age of egalitarianism it may be suggested that the concept of a calling creates and maintains the division between clergy and laity, or exaggerates the distinction and therefore should not be applied to today. It may be worthwhile noting also that the more liberal pastor does not operate from a sense of having been called by God and sent by heaven. For some preachers, the pulpit is no more than a springboard to jump off into other fields. Thus some men who were never called admit it, claiming they felt led to enter the ministry because it offered the best platform for instituting economic, racial, political and social programs.

Those "not sent but who just went" can never experience the joy of having had a supernatural call into a supernatural ministry, or the joy of answering that calling, no matter how successful they may be from man's point of view. The calling to the Christian ministry is one of grace. That God would put His hands on a piece of clay and put within that frail, earthen vessel the treasure of the gospel of the shed blood of Jesus Christ—the thought is humbling!

Let the reader ponder: Do you delight in the study of God's Word, the Bible? Do you have the ability to communicate? Are you willing to live a life of discipline? Is there the "fire shut up in your bones" conviction that you must preach? Has God given confirming evidence in the fruit of your labor? Are others convinced of your calling and have confirmed it by opening doors for you to exercise your gifts?

PREACHER PITFALLS

"Smite the shepherd and scatter the sheep"—this, in order to strike at the Savior, is still the strategy of Satan! There are many pitfalls, traps or hidden dangers in the Christian ministry, and to be forewarned is to be forearmed.

ARROGANCE: The preacher who thinks too highly of himself because of his singing ability, looks, wealth, education and degrees, etc., is not a good pastoral model. Puffed-up-ness leads to down-fall-ness! (Rom. 12:3; 1 Cor. 1:26–29, 10:12; Prov. 16:18; 3 John 9; Isa. 42:8).

Closely related is STUBBORNNESS, especially over issues which are not really that important. The preacher who majors in minors undermines his ministry and messes up the message the Master called him to preach.

Another close relative is ARGUMENTATIVENESS. The preacher who enjoys conflict is headed for a stormy pastorate. And if he is called to a "fighting" church he is in for trouble.

BURDEN–BEARING: There is the realization that the preacher's ego may lead him into the trap of maintaining a heavy counseling schedule.

LAZINESS can ruin your ministry. The lack of industriousness may show itself in poor visitation of the shut-in and sick, and by overlooking the discouraged in the congregation. It may show itself also in the lack of preparation of sermons. Failure to make preaching central is quite in contrast to that attitude expressed by Paul when he said, "For Christ did not send me to baptize, but to preach the gospel" (1 Cor. 1:17).

This brings to mind also what may be called LOPSIDEDNESS. Here the lazy preacher is guilty of riding a hobbyhorse, going off on a tangent, and using the same book of the Bible or the Gospels, for example, for sermons Sunday after Sunday, instead of providing members with the variety which constitutes the Word of God: fire, meat, water, hammer, sword, honey, light, milk, etc. This is not, however, to preclude preaching series of messages from certain books of the Bible, or on certain themes.

RESPECT OF PERSONS: The fear of man is indeed a snare (Prov. 29:25; 1 Sam. 15:24; Gal. 2:12–14; Jer. 1:7–9; Ezek. 2:6–7).

FAVORITISM: Do not let close friendship with certain church members rob other members of the time necessary for you to spend with them.

PLEASING EVERYBODY of course is impossible; it is an unrealistic goal, so don't even try it. The attempt to please everybody easily leads to compromise of doctrine and deed. Read *Aesop's Fables*, "The Miller, His Son and Their Donkey." Seek instead to please the Lord Jesus Christ.

CONFIDENTIALITY: Even though counseling may be but a small part of your total ministry, without confidentiality even that will not be effective. I cringe when I hear pastors use illustrations based upon their counseling sessions. At all costs keep confidentiality—keep secret that which is shared with you.

ADMINISTRATIVE CONTROL: Spend time on administration. Failure to do so cuts your effectiveness in other pastoral roles. Every pastor is a bishop, an overseer; this means you have the responsibility of supervising the entire program of the church.

It does not mean you attempt to do all the work. God has given gifts to all His saints. Nor does it mean to "lord it over those entrusted to you." Men who attempt to be dictators stunt the spiritual growth of their congregations and disobey the Word of God (1 Pet. 5:3). They run the risk of quenching the Holy Spirit and of sowing the seeds of unrest and rebellion.

Finally, be careful in your relationships with the WOMEN in the church and with MONEY. A word to the wise is sufficient. These are two areas which have caused many ministers to fall. Be aware of it.

THE APOSTLES' CREED

The Apostles' Creed is a statement of basic Christian beliefs. Although brief so far as the number of words it contains, it is grand as to the weight of its teachings (*brevis et grandis*: Augustine). It was prepared by unknown parties (certainly not by the Apostles) perhaps as early as 150 AD. The form used by the Roman Catholic Church has "Creator" for "Maker," "died" for "dead," "living" for "quick," capitalizes "Holy Catholic Church," and contains several other very minor differences in punctuation.

"I believe in God, the Father Almighty, Maker of heaven and earth; and in Jesus Christ, His only Son, our Lord; who was conceived by the Holy Ghost, born of the Virgin Mary, suffered under Pontius Pilate, was crucified, dead, and buried; He descended into hell*; the third day He rose again from the dead. He ascended into heaven, and sitteth on the right hand of God the Father Almighty; from thence He shall come to judge the quick and the dead. I believe in the Holy Ghost; the holy catholic† church; the communion of saints; the forgiveness of sins; the resurrection of the body; and the life everlasting. Amen."

---

* or, Hades; or, He went to the place of departed spirits
† or, Christian

Baptism

FORMULA

"My brother (sister), it is with joy and delight, in obedience to the Bible, that I now baptize you 'in the name of the Father, and of the Son, and of the Holy Spirit'" (Matt. 28:19).

If salvation depends upon what is spoken over the candidate at baptism, then men are saved by works and not by grace. How sad then to encounter preachers who argue that the only formula to be used in baptizing candidates is found in Acts 2:38, and that unless the words "I baptize you in the name of Jesus Christ" are spoken the candidate is not saved.

Water baptism is an outward sign of an inward change; it is a symbol of identification, a public confession of faith. The formula used does not produce any change of heart. To argue that Matthew 28:19 is never mentioned in the book of Acts is to argue from silence. We do not know what words were spoken in the baptisms recorded there.

In Acts 8:16 we read, "baptized in the name of the Lord Jesus." In Acts 8:36 no name is mentioned at all. In Acts 10:48 it is "in the name of the Lord," which is, of course, "Jesus Christ." In Acts 16:33 no name is given. And in Acts 19:5, it is "in the name of the Lord Jesus." So that even if we were to take these as the exact words spoken during the ceremony, the variations deny settling on Acts 2:38 as the formula.

The fact is, we are not told in the book of Acts what words were spoken during the baptisms. Remember that in Acts 2 Peter's entire audience was Jewish—men of Israel, including proselytes. It was desired that they change their minds, repent concerning their attitudes about Jesus Christ. The "name" of Jesus Christ represents all that He is, all that He has done. To be baptized in such a name means then to acknowledge all that He is; it is to recognize His authority and power. Emphasis is not upon what words were spoken; rather, emphasis is upon the act of baptizing, for it represents what the Lord Jesus has done already to the believer.

I.M. Haldeman said: "The record in the book of Acts of certain persons who were baptized in the name of Jesus Christ is simply the declaration that they were baptized upon a confession of their faith in Him not merely as Jesus Christ, but as the Son of God" (Acts 8:37). This certainly is the teaching intended for the nations or Gentiles of Matthew 28:19. It is impossible to make a saving confession of Jesus Christ as the Son of God without recognizing the participation of the Trinity. There is a unity in the Godhead that is expressed throughout the earthly ministry of our Lord. And we should not use a baptism formula that ignores the Trinity. Thus the formula in Matthew 28:19 is not "in the names" (plural), but "in the name" (singular), of the Father, and of the Son, and of the Holy Spirit.

Father, Son and Holy Spirit participated in the conception, birth and incarnation; they took part in our Lord's earthly ministry, His sacrificial death, resurrection and the way of salvation through faith in His shed blood. And if there is any one place we have a clear picture of the Trinity, it is at the baptism of Jesus Christ, the Son of God (Matt. 3:16–17; Mark 1:9–11; Luke 3:22; John 1:32–34).

IMMERSION

A minister preached a sermon in which he attempted to show that "in" and "into" did not mean immersion. He said; "John did not baptize the Lord Jesus in the Jordan, but close to, near by, round about Jordan. Philip and the Ethiopian eunuch did not go down into the water, but close to, near by, round about."

At the conclusion of the sermon, one of the visitors in the congregation stood up and said, "Reverend, your sermon today has brought me much comfort. It explains many mysteries to me, things which have long perplexed me. For one thing, I could never understand how Jonah could live in the belly of that great fish for three days and three nights. Now I see that he was not in the fish, but close to, near by, round about, swimming in the water. And the Bible says that the three Hebrew boys were cast into the fiery furnace, and I wondered how in the world they lived. You have explained it. They were not actually in the furnace but close to, near by, round about, where they could warm themselves. We read that Daniel was cast into the den of lions, and why those beasts did not devour him was a mystery to me. But he was not in the den at all, but only close to, near by, round about where he could hear them roar and feel no harm.

"And then, Reverend, I am a very wicked man and have long been afraid of future punishment. You have relieved my apprehension. When the Bible says the wicked shall be cast into hell with all the nations that forget God, I shall henceforth interpret it as meaning that I shall not actually go to hell, but only close to, near by, round about."

BAPTIST DISTINCTIVES

1. BIBLE: The Word of God is our standard of faith and final authority.
2. MEMBERSHIP: We believe in a regenerated membership, believers only.
3. BAPTISM: By immersion, infant baptism is rejected.
4. SCRIPTURAL OFFICERS: Pastor and Deacons only.
5. ORDINANCES: Baptism and the Lord's Supper (Communion).
6. POLITY or GOVERNMENT: Congregational, autonomous, sovereign. Each Baptist church is independent of the other; majority rule.
7. SEPARATION OF CHURCH AND STATE: No local Baptist assembly is to be supported by the State or dictated to by the State in matters of faith and practice.
8. MISSIONARY: We are obligated to evangelize.

Benedictions

Num. 6:24–26: The Lord bless you, and keep you; the Lord make His face shine upon you, and be gracious to you; the Lord lift up His countenance upon you, and give you peace.

1 Kings 8:57–58: May the Lord our God be with us . . . that He may incline our hearts to Himself, to walk in all His ways, and to keep His commandments. . . .

Ps. 19:14: Let the words of my mouth, and the meditation of my heart be acceptable in Your sight, O Lord, my strength and my Redeemer.

Ps. 24:4–5: He who has clean hands and a pure heart, who has not lifted up his soul to an idol, nor sworn deceitfully; he shall receive blessing from the Lord, and righteousness from the God of his salvation.

Ps. 67:1–2: God be merciful to us and bless us, and cause His face to shine upon us . . . that Your way may be known on earth, Your salvation among all nations.

Acts 20:32: I commend you to God and to the word of His grace, which is able to build you up and give you an inheritance among all those who are sanctified.

Rom. 15:5–6: May the God of patience and comfort grant you to be like-minded toward one another, according to Christ Jesus, that you may with one mind and one mouth glorify the God and Father of our Lord Jesus Christ.

Rom. 15:13: Now may the God of hope fill you with all joy and peace in believing, that you may abound in hope by the power of the Holy Spirit.

Rom. 15:33: Now the God of peace be with you all. Amen.

Rom. 16:24, 27: The grace of our Lord Jesus Christ be with you all. Amen. To God, alone wise, be glory through Jesus Christ forever. Amen. (1 Thess. 5:28; 2 Thess. 3:18; Phil. 4:23; Rev. 22:21)

1 Cor. 1:3: Grace to you and peace from God our Father and the Lord Jesus Christ.

2 Cor. 13:14: The grace of the Lord Jesus Christ, and the love of God, and the communion of the Holy Spirit be with you all. Amen.

Gal. 6:18: Brethren, the grace of our Lord Jesus Christ be with your spirit. Amen.

Eph. 3:20–21: Now to Him who is able to do exceedingly abundantly above all that we ask or think, according to the power that works in us, to Him be glory in the church by Christ Jesus to all generations, forever and ever. Amen.

Eph. 6:23–24: Peace to the brethren, and love with faith, from God the Father and the Lord Jesus Christ. Grace be with all those who love our Lord Jesus Christ in sincerity. Amen.

Phil. 4:6–7: Be anxious for nothing, but in everything by prayer and supplication, with thanksgiving, let your requests be made known to God; and the peace of God, which surpasses all understanding, will guard your hearts and minds through Christ Jesus.

1 Thess. 5:23: Now may the God of peace Himself sanctify you completely; and may your whole spirit, soul, and body be preserved blameless at the coming of our Lord Jesus Christ.

2 Thess. 2:6–17: Now may our Lord Jesus Christ Himself, and our God and Father, who has loved us and given us everlasting consolation and good hope by grace, comfort your hearts and establish you in every good word and work.

1 Tim. 1:17: Now to the King eternal, immortal, invisible, to God who alone is wise, be honor and glory forever and ever. Amen.

2 Tim. 4:22: The Lord Jesus Christ be with your spirit. Grace be with you. Amen.

Philem. 25: The grace of the Lord Jesus Christ be with your spirit. Amen.

Heb. 13:20–21: Now may the God of peace who brought up our Lord Jesus from the dead, that great Shepherd of the sheep, through the blood of the everlasting covenant, make you complete in every good work to do His will, working in you what is well pleasing in His sight, through Jesus Christ, to whom be glory forever and ever. Amen.

Phil. 4:20: Now to our God and Father be glory forever and ever. Amen.

1 Pet. 5:10–11: But may the God of all grace, who called us to His eternal glory by Christ Jesus, after you have suffered a while, perfect, establish, strengthen, and settle you. To Him be the glory and the dominion forever and ever. Amen.

1 Pet. 5:14b: Peace to you all who are in Christ Jesus. Amen.

2 Pet. 3:18: But grow in the grace and knowledge of our Lord and Savior Jesus Christ. To Him be the glory both now and forever. Amen.

Jude 24–25: Now to Him who is able to keep you from stumbling, and to present you faultless before the presence of His glory with exceeding joy, to God our Savior, who alone is wise, be glory and majesty, dominion and power, both now and forever. Amen.

Note: The *Mizpah*, "The Lord watch between you and me, when we are absent one from another" (Genesis 31:49), should not be used as a benediction, although God's care is commendable and desirable. However, the context has to do with lying, cheating, swindling. Based upon their prior experiences with one another, Laban and Jacob did not trust each other. These words were spoken in exhortation and warning to behave properly. Laban was concerned with Jacob's treatment of his daughters whom Jacob had married.

Bible

BECOMING A BETTER BIBLE STUDENT

1. PRAYER: Always pray before beginning Bible study. Ask for the guidance of the Holy Spirit your Teacher.
2. BIBLE: Believe that the Bible *is* the Word of God. Ignore theories teaching (1) the Bible contains God's Word, or (2) becomes God's Word. The Bible *is* the Word of God whether men believe it or not.
3. CHRIST–CENTEREDNESS: Jesus Christ is the scarlet thread that runs throughout the Bible—Genesis to Revelation. No matter what the text, it has relevance always to Jesus Christ who shed His blood at Calvary.
4. CONTEXT: Always study the verses before and after the particular verse considered. At times it may be necessary to read the entire chapter to see where one verse fits. To answer a question about verse five you should read verses four and six before venturing an answer.
5. DISPENSATIONS: God does different things at different times. Do not confuse the era called the Law (Moses to Calvary) with the era called the Church Age (Pentecost to Rapture), or the era immediately following called the

Tribulation, or the era called the Kingdom Age (Millennium: 1,000 years following the Tribulation). Seek to know the time frames of the Bible passages you study.

6. ISRAEL: Do not spiritualize away Israel and make Israel the Church. The Jews are still on this planet earth, and God's promises to that nation will be kept literally, completely. The Church has not taken Israel's place! Israel has never occupied all the land God promised her.

7. POSITION AND CONDITION: Some verses in the New Testament describe our position with God, the way He looks at us through the eyes of Jesus Christ. Positionally we are perfect; this is our standing. But our condition, the way we actually are in our experience, is something else. Indeed, our state is far from perfect. For example: Positionally we cannot practice sin (1 John 3:9). Such is our standing before God that it is impossible for us to habitually, consistently, whole-heartedly sin. Conditionally, if we say we have no sin nature we deceive ourselves and lie (1 John 1:8). Our state or condition is such that we need an advocate (1 John 2:1).

THE MIRROR OF THE BIBLE (JAMES 1:22–25)

The Bible's candid description of man helps convince us it is the Word of God—a God who knows us and "tells it like it is." It is not a mirror reflecting a distorted image as in a "Fun House" at the amusement park. Man is portrayed as having the throat of an open sepulcher, a tongue full of guile, snake poison under his lips, a mouth full of cursing and bitterness, feet swift to shed innocent blood, eyes full of lust, a heart that is deceitful and incurably sick, a hard head, shoulders unwilling to bear responsibility and a back fit for a strap. No matter who you are, your picture is reflected. Look in the mirror and see someone who is:

A conspirator like Absalom
Weak like King Ahab
Evil as Alexander the coppersmith
Treacherous as the Amalekites
Stubborn as Balaam
An insurrectionist like Barabbas
Blind as Bartimaeus
A desecrator like Belshazzar
Murderous at heart like Cain
Shameless as Canaan
Cruel as the Chaldeans
Rebellious as Dathan and Abiram
An adulterer as was David
Deceptive as Delilah
Worldly as Demas
A "Big Deal" like Diotrephes
Callous as Dives*
Carnal as Esau
A sleepyhead like Eutychus
Greedy as Gehazi
A godless giant like Goliath
Full of hatred like Haman

* The rich man (Luke 16:19)

A killer of babies like Herod the Great
  Vengeful as Herodias
    Murmuring like the Israelites in the wilderness
    Full of trickery like Jannes and Jambres
      Painted like Jezebel
        A swindler like Jacob
          Traitorous as Judas
            Poor as Lazarus
              Ungrateful as the nine cleansed lepers
                Proud as Naaman
                  Boastful as Nebuchadnezzar
                    Drunk like Noah
                      Impetuous as Simon Peter
                        Hard-hearted as the Pharaoh of Egypt
                          Hypocritical like the Pharisees
                            Cynical as Pontius Pilate
                            Lustful as Potiphar's wife
                          Blasphemous as the Rabshakeh of Assyria
                        A prostitute like Rahab
                      Sorrowful as the rich young ruler
                    Living in common-law like the Samaritan woman
                  Physically strong, morally weak as Samson
                Contemptuous as Sanballat
              A church-hater as was Saul of Tarsus
            Disobedient as king Saul
          Pessimist like Thomas
        A little sinner like Zacchaeus

For all such, the Son of Man came to seek and to save:
Luke 19:10.

HOW TO USE THE BIBLE

Prayerfully: Always begin your sermons, Bible study, lectures, etc., with prayer. Ask the Lord's blessing upon your efforts and for Holy Spirit guidance.

Christologically: See Jesus Christ. Never fail to relate the Bible passage to Him. Not just tail-stuck-on-the-donkey fashion, but in a meaningful, appropriate, relevant manner. Whatever the Bible verse deals with—Aaron to Zacchaeus—see Christ! After all, He is the Word!

Diligently: Stick with it, persevere, keep at it. In time you will find the Holy Spirit has made a Bible computer out of your brain. Memorize scriptures, store them in your heart (Ps. 119:11). And see to it that Bibles are supplied to the members of your church.

Contextually: Bible verses taken out of context may be used to prove anything under the sun. Sometimes man-made chapter divisions will lead you astray (e.g., Matt. 16:28–17:1).

Confidently: This calls for belief in verbal inspiration of the Scriptures (2 Tim. 3:16–17).

Believe it will do what God sends it out to do (Isa. 55:11)
Believe that it *is* the Word of God (1 Thess. 2:13).

23

Believe that it is what it says it is:
    (1) a lamp, light (Ps. 119:105)
    (2) a fire (Jer. 5:14; 20:9)
    (3) a hammer (Jer. 23:29[fire also])
    (4) eternal (Isa. 40:8; Mark 13:1)
    (5) food (1 Pet. 2:2; Job 23:12; Jer. 15:16; Ps. 119:103)
    (6) a sword (Heb. 4:12; Eph. 6:17)
    (7) truth (John 17:17; Ps. 119:160)
    (8) pure (Ps. 119:140)

Believe that it is doing and shall accomplish what it says:
    (1) sanctify (John 17:17; 1 Tim. 4:5)
    (2) cleanse (Ps. 119:9; John 15:3)
    (3) regenerate (1 Pet. 1:23)
    (4) sustain life (Matt. 4:4; Deut. 8:3)
    (5) instruct (Rom. 15:4; 2 Tim. 3:16–17)
    (6) admonish [put into mind] (1 Cor. 10:11)

Gratefully: With gratitude. Thank God for the Bible, for in it He has revealed His mind (1 Cor. 2:11; 2 Pet. 1:20–21). Approximately 40 different men, covering a period of some 1,600 years, wrote the 66 books. (Old Testament: 1,110 years, intertestamental gap; 400 years; New Testament: 100 years). God preserved copies of copies of copies and pieces of copies throughout the years, then raised up scholars, men and women, gifted in languages, to work with the manuscripts (as the manuscripts were discovered).

We believe today that we have 999 of every 1,000 original words. For those whose eyes were put out, hands chopped off, who lost their lives, were burned alive at the stake, beheaded—for daring to translate, write, print, preach, publish, distribute the Bible—we say, "Thank the Lord!"

The Book of Books is bathed in blood. And Christians ought to be aware of the grace of God in our land. Furthermore, the Bible is an expression of the love of God—a God who would not have us to be ignorant, but wants us to know more about Him. And rest assured, the more we learn of Him the more we will love Him!

BIBLE CHARGE—AT AN INSTALLATION

Let others believe that the Bible *contains* the Word of God and thereby exalt themselves as they determine what to keep and what to discard. Let others hold that the Bible *becomes* the Word of God, so they can pick and choose, and live in their pet sins. Let others believe that the Bible is fallible because it came through fallen man. Their mistake is to ignore the Bible's claim that holy men of old were superintended by the Holy Spirit. While others grope in darkness, you hold high the Word which is both a lamp and a light.

While others fight with the carnal weapons and power movements of this world, you continue to use the Sword of the Spirit. Study it, use it prayerfully, and you will find it still conquers Satanic strongholds; it still convicts and converts; it still regenerates hearts; it still comforts the distraught; it is still a fire and a hammer!

Live the Word and continue to lift high the Bible and its message of the shed blood of God's dear Son, the Lord Jesus Christ. And when this life is over and your ministry here is ended, may it be yours to hear the Word-Made-Flesh say, "Well done, good and faithful servant. Well done!"

TRADITIONAL "SAYINGS"

1. It is incorrect to say, "You must be *worthy* to take the Lord's Supper" (1 Cor. 11:27–29). The word *unworthily* is an adverb modifying the verbs to eat and to drink. It thus refers to the manner in which we partake of the Supper. If it were *unworthy*, nobody would qualify. But the emphasis is upon conduct, not character. Paul was concerned with those Christians who celebrated it in a careless, irreverent spirit. Pastors must warn members not to take Communion with levity, gum-chewing, flippancy, glibness, indifference or irreverence. We are to examine ourselves (*dokimazo*: prove, test, in order to approve); test our attitudes with an eye to approval. And remember, there are no excuses for not taking the Lord's Supper. Examine yourself and eat!

2. "Lord, don't let my sins meet me at the judgment bar!" All of the sins of the believer—past, present and future—have been washed away by the blood of the Lord Jesus Christ. We either believe this or we don't. According to the Bible God has done the following with our sins: (1) Blotted them out (Isa. 44:22; Acts 3:19), (2) Remembered them no more (Isa. 43:25), (3) Forgiven them (Eph. 4:32; Matt.

26:28), (4) Removed them as far as the east is from the west (Ps. 103:12), (5) Cast them behind His back (Isa. 38:17), (6) Covered them (Ps. 32:1) and (7) Has cleansed or washed us (Rev. 1:5). We must learn to take God at His Word and not pray contrary to what the Bible teaches. Our salvation is complete in Jesus Christ.

3. "Well, you know, a little child shall lead them." This is sometimes said when a little child is used of God to win his mother or father to the Lord. But Isaiah 11:6 describes the kingdom age, the millennial age. At that time there will be no wild animals in the earth. Creatures formerly wild and ferocious, or poisonous, will be at peace, and little children shall play with them without fear or harm.

4. "I woke up this morning, clothed in my right mind. . . ." The demoniac at Gadara is described as (1) living in the tombs, and not in a house, (2) exceedingly fierce, (3) preventing people from passing by that way, (4) with superhuman strength breaking fetters and chains, (5) he could not be tamed, (6) went screaming and crying out, (7) cut himself with stones, (8) was restless, running here and there day and night, (9) "And he wore no clothes" (Luke 8:27). Prior to healing, the man ran around naked; but when the Lord Jesus healed him the man put on clothing. Note the comma after the word "clothed" (v. 35).

5. "Let's give the benediction. Now may the Lord watch between me and thee when we are absent one from another. Amen." Jacob and Laban did not trust each other. To see why, read

Genesis chapters 29–31. The heap of stone was erected as a witness of Jacob's covenant with Laban and, from Laban's point of view, serves as a reminder that God was watching the way Jacob would treat Leah and Rachel, Laban's daughters whom Jacob had married. In short, the *Mizpah* speaks of suspicion, lack of trust between Jacob and Laban. A threat is implied. Should then the *Mizpah* be used as a benediction?

6. "Lord give us a home in heaven, where the wicked cease from troubling, and our weary souls shall find rest" (Job 3:17). Job wished he had never been born; this was a typical way of expressing despair (cf. Jer. 20:14–18; Job 3:3–4, 9–10). He wished he had died at birth (Job 3:11–19). Such was his misery that death would have been a sweet relief, an escape from life's agony. In death's dormitory kings, statesmen and princes, as well as prisoners, were at ease and slaves freed from their toil. And so it is in the grave (not heaven) that the wicked cease from raging, stop their evil. In the grave Job felt he would find relief from human troublers. And whereas it is true there will be no wicked ones in heaven troubling us, and in heaven we shall be at rest, the context of Job 3:17 does not support making this "place" heaven. For Job it is the grave.

Call to Worship: Invocations

Gen. 28:17: How awesome is this place! This is none other than the house of God, and this is the gate of heaven!

Josh. 24:14-15: Now therefore, fear the Lord, serve Him in sincerity and in truth, and put away the gods which your fathers served on the other side of the River and in Egypt. Serve the Lord! And if it seems evil to you to serve the Lord, choose for yourselves this day whom you will serve, whether the gods which your fathers served that were on the other side of the River, or the gods of the Amorites, in whose land you dwell. But as for me and my house, we will serve the Lord.

Ps. 19:14: Let the words of my mouth and the meditation of my heart be acceptable in Your sight, O Lord, my strength and my Redeemer.

Ps. 24:1, 9–10: The earth is the Lord's and all its fullness, the world and those who dwell therein. . . . Lift up your heads, O you gates! Lift up, you everlasting doors! And the King of glory shall come in. Who is this King of glory? The Lord of hosts, He is the King of glory.

Ps. 24:3–4: Who may ascend into the hill of the Lord? Or who may stand in His holy place? He who has clean hands and a pure heart, who has not lifted up his soul to an idol, nor sworn deceitfully.

Ps. 27:4,14: One thing I have desired of the Lord, that will I seek: that I may dwell in the house of the Lord all the days of my life, to behold the beauty of the Lord, and to inquire in His temple. . . . Wait on the Lord; be of good courage, and He shall strengthen your heart. Wait, I say, on the Lord!

Ps. 29:2: Give unto the Lord the glory due to His name; worship the Lord in the beauty of holiness.

Ps. 34:1–3; 1 Chron. 16:25: I will bless the Lord at all times; His praise shall continually be in my mouth. My soul shall make its boast in the Lord; the humble shall hear of it and be glad. Oh, magnify the Lord with me, and let us exalt His name together. . . . For the Lord is great and greatly to be praised.

Ps. 46:10: Be still, and know that I am God; I will be exalted among the nations, I will be exalted in the earth!

Ps. 55:22: Cast your burden on the Lord, and He shall sustain you; He shall never permit the righteous to be moved.

Ps. 84:2: My soul longs, yes, even faints for the courts of the Lord; my heart and my flesh cry out for the living God.

Ps. 91:1–2: He who dwells in the secret place of the Most High shall abide under the shadow of the Almighty. I will say of the Lord, "He is my refuge and my fortress; my God, in Him I will trust."

Ps. 95:6–7: Oh come, let us worship and bow down; let us kneel before the Lord our Maker. For He is our God, and we are the people of His pasture, and the sheep of His hand.

Ps. 96:1–2,4: Oh, sing to the Lord a new song! Sing to the Lord, all the earth. Sing to the Lord, bless His name; proclaim the good news of His salvation from day to day. For the Lord is great and greatly to be praised.

Ps. 96:1, 3, 8–9: Oh, sing to the Lord a new song! Sing to the Lord, all the earth. . . . Declare His glory among the nations, His wonders among all peoples. . . . Give to the Lord the glory due His name; bring an offering, and come into His courts! Oh, worship the Lord in the beauty of holiness!

Ps. 99:9: Exalt the Lord our God, and worship at His holy hill; for the Lord our God is holy.

Ps. 100: Make a joyful shout to the Lord, all you lands! Serve the Lord with gladness; come before His presence with singing. Know that the Lord, He is God; it is He who has made us, and not we ourselves; we are His people and the sheep of His pasture. Enter into His gates with thanksgiving, and into His courts with praise. Be thankful to Him, and bless His name. For the Lord is good; His mercy is everlasting, and His truth endures to all generations.

Ps. 107:1–2: Oh, give thanks to the Lord, for He is good! For His mercy endures forever. Let the redeemed of the Lord say so, whom He has redeemed from the hand of the enemy.

Ps. 111:1–2: Praise the Lord! I will praise the Lord with my whole heart, in the assembly of the upright and in the congregation. The works of the Lord are great, studied by all who have pleasure in them.

Ps. 118:24: This is the day the Lord has made; we will rejoice and be glad in it.

Ps. 121:1–2: I will lift up my eyes to the hills—From whence comes my help? My help comes from the Lord, who made heaven and earth.

Ps. 122:1: I was glad when they said to me, "Let us go into the house of the Lord."

Ps. 124:8: Our help is in the name of the Lord, who made heaven and earth.

Ps. 150: Praise the Lord! Praise God in His sanctuary; praise Him in His mighty firmament! Praise Him for His mighty acts; praise Him according to His excellent greatness! Praise Him with the sound of the trumpet; praise Him with the lute and harp! Praise Him with the timbrel and dance; praise Him with stringed instruments and flutes! Praise him with loud cymbals; praise Him with clashing cymbals! Let everything that has breath praise the Lord. Praise the Lord!

Ps. 145:18–19: The Lord is near to all who call upon Him, to all who call upon Him in truth. He will fulfill the desire of those who fear Him; He also will hear their cry and save them.

Prov. 3:5–6: Trust in the Lord with all your heart, and lean not on your own understanding; in all your ways acknowledge Him, and He shall direct your paths.

Isa. 6:3; Ps. 95:6: Holy, holy, holy is the Lord of hosts; the whole earth is full of His glory! . . . Oh come, let us worship and bow down; let us kneel before the Lord our Maker.

Isa. 33:2: O Lord, be gracious to us; we have waited for You. Be our arm every morning, our salvation also in the time of trouble.

Isa. 40:28–31: Have you not known? Have you not heard? The everlasting God, the Lord, the Creator of the ends of the earth, neither faints nor is weary. His understanding is unsearchable. He gives power to the weak, and to those who have no might He increases strength. Even the youths shall faint and be weary, and the young men shall utterly fall, but those who wait on the Lord shall renew their strength; they shall mount up with wings like eagles, they shall run and not be weary, they shall walk and not faint.

Isa. 55:1,6: Ho! Everyone who thirsts, come to the waters; and you who have no money, come, buy and eat. Yes, come, buy wine and milk without money and without price. . . . Seek the Lord while He may be found, call upon Him while He is near. (Dr. Chafer cautions us not to use Isaiah 55:6 as an invitation to unbelievers, for the unregenerate do not seek the Lord—Romans 3:11).

Hab. 2:20: But the Lord is in His holy temple. Let all the earth keep silence before Him. (We are reminded that this verse is fulfilled only during the Millennium.)

Matt. 7:7–8: Ask, and it will be given to you; seek, and you will find; knock, and it will be opened to you. For everyone who asks receives, and he who seeks finds, and to him who knocks it will be opened.

Matt. 11:28–30: Come to Me, all you who labor and are heavy laden, and I will give you rest. Take My yoke upon you and learn from Me, for I am gentle and lowly in heart, and you will find rest for your souls. For My yoke is easy and My burden is light.

John 4:23–24: But the hour is coming, and now is, when the true worshipers will worship the Father in spirit and truth; for the Father is seeking such to worship Him. God is spirit, and those who worship Him must worship in spirit and truth.

Rom. 12:1–2: I beseech you therefore, brethren, by the mercies of God, that you present your bodies a living sacrifice, holy, acceptable to God, which is your reasonable service. And do not be conformed to this world, but be transformed by the renewing of your mind, that you may prove what is that good and acceptable and perfect will of God.

James 4:8, 10: Draw near to God and He will draw near to you. . . . Humble yourselves in the sight of the Lord, and He will lift you up.

Rev. 3:20; Matt. 7:7: Behold, I stand at the door and knock. If anyone hears My voice and opens the door, I will come in to him and dine with him, and he with Me. . . . Ask, and it will be given to you; seek, and you will find; knock, and it will be opened to you.

Choir-Chorus Anniversary: Sermon Texts

Exod. 15:1: Song of Victory
Exod. 15:2: Strength, Song, Salvation (Ps. 118:14)
Ps. 81:1; 95:1: A Joyful Noise
Ps. 137:3–4: A Song of Zion
Isa. 30:29: A Song in the Night (Job 35:10; Ps. 42:8; 77:6).
Acts 16:25: A Song at Midnight
1 Cor. 14:15: How to Sing
Eph. 5:19: Singing on the Inside!
Col. 3:16: Singing Spiritual Songs
James 5:13: Sing for Joy!
Rev. 5:9: A New Song (Rev. 14:3; Ps. 33:3, 40:3, 96:1, 98:1, 144:9, 149:1)

Christ

WHAT HAPPENED AT CALVARY

God the Son became a Man in order to die. That death, incomprehensible to man, presents us with a number of paradoxes, truths seemingly contradictory. We can say that at that moment when Christ was smitten, it was as if the—

Advocate was judged by men
Almighty One was humbled
Blessed One became a Curse
Bread of Life was swallowed up
Chief Cornerstone was moved out of place
Creator was crucified by creatures
Door was slammed shut
Gates of the City of Refuge were closed
Great Physician was stricken
Healer was made Pain
Helping Hand was cruelly spiked
Judge of the world was condemned
Just One was made Guilt
Lamb was made a Scapegoat
Liberator was shackled to a cross

Light of the world was snuffed out
Lion of Judah was tamed
Love was hated
Majesty was deposed
Morning Star was hidden
Prince of Life was slain
Redeemer was rejected
Rock of ages was shattered
Rose of Sharon was plucked
Savior became Lostness
Seed of the Woman was bruised
Sinless One was made Sin
Son was forsaken by God
Spotless Lamb became blemished
Sun of Righteousness was eclipsed
Truth was called a Liar
War was declared on the Prince of Peace
Well of Water dried up
Word was censored

WHAT CHRIST ENDURED

"Endured the cross, despising the shame . . . endured such contradiction of sinners against Himself" (Heb. 12:2–3, KJV).

1. Tested by the Devil in the wilderness (Matt. 4)
2. Came unto His own, they received Him not (John 1:11)
3. Rejecters at Nazareth tried to throw Him over a cliff (Luke 4:29)

4. Accused of blasphemy for telling palsied man, "Your sins are forgiven" (Matt. 9:3)

5. Castigated, targeted for murder because He healed a man at the pool of Bethesda on the Sabbath (John 5:10)

6. Chastised because His disciples did not fast (Mark 2:18)

7. Sought to kill Him because He made Himself equal with God the Father (John 5:18)

8. Complained because His disciples plucked grain on the Sabbath (Mark 2:24)

9. Called a law breaker for healing on the Sabbath (Matt. 12:13)

10. Religious leaders plotted to destroy Him (Matt. 12:14)

11. Asked to leave town by hog owners (Matt. 8:34)

12. Criticized for eating with tax collectors and sinners (Matt. 9:11)

13. Laughed to scorn for saying a girl was not dead but asleep (Matt. 9:24)

14. Accused of casting out demons through the prince of demons (Matt. 9:34)

15. Despised because He was a carpenter (Mark 6:3)

16. Unbelief at Nazareth limited His mighty works (Matt. 13:58)

17. His disciples accused of transgressing tradition for not washing their hands when they ate bread (Matt. 15:2)

18. Taunted by sign-seekers (Matt. 16:1)

19. "Do You pay taxes?" asked the tax collectors (Matt. 17:24)

20. His own brothers did not believe in Him (John 7:5)

21. Accused of deceiving the people (John 7:12)

22. Said to be possessed by a demon (John 7:20)
23. Officers sent to take Him, but failed (John 7:32,45)
24. Woman caught in adultery brought to Him to test Him (John 8:3)
25. Accused of tooting His own horn; told His witness was not true: for He said, "I am the Light of the World" (John 8:12–13)
26. They insinuated His birth was illegitimate: "We were not born of fornication!" (John 8:41)
27. They picked up stones to kill Him for saying, "Before Abraham was, I am" (John 8:59)
28. Called crazy, beside Himself (John 10:20)
29. Sought to stone Him to death because He said, "I and My Father are One" (John 10:31)
30. After Lazarus was raised, they took counsel to put Christ to death, and to kill Lazarus (John 11:53)
31. They were indignant because the woman bent over for 18 years was healed on the Sabbath (Luke 13:14)
32. Derided by the Pharisees because of the parable concerning the steward (Luke 16:14)
33. Tested about divorce: "Moses said . . . what do You say?" (Matt. 19:3)
34. Murmured against because He went to be a guest of Zacchaeus (Luke 19:7)
35. His authority was challenged (Matt. 21:23)
36. They sought to destroy Him after He cleansed the Temple a second time (Mark 11:18)

37. Tried to entangle Him in His talk (Matt. 22:15)
38. Sought to get Him into trouble with the Roman Government by testing Him: "Is it lawful to give taxes to Caesar?" (Matt. 22:17)
39. A woman married seven brothers; which one will be her husband in the Resurrection? inquired the deceitful Sadducees (Matt. 22:23)
40. He was betrayed by Judas (Matt. 26:14; Ps. 41:9)
41. Hated by the world (John 15:18; 7:7)
42. Arrested as a common criminal (Matt. 26:47; Mark 14:46)
43. Forsaken and deserted (Matt. 26:56)
44. Denied by Simon Peter (Mark 14:68–72)
45. False witnesses spoke against Him (Matt. 26:59)
46. At the interview before Caiaphas, an officer struck Him with the palm of his hand (John 18:22)
47. Accused of blasphemy by Caiaphas the high priest (Matt. 26:65)
48. They spat in His face (Matt. 26:67)
49. He was buffeted while His face was covered (Matt. 26:67; Mark 14:65)
50. They smote Him with the palms of their hands (Matt. 26:67)
51. Again He was mocked (Matt. 26:68)
52. Once more they plotted to kill Him (Matt. 27:1)
53. Liars told Pilate Christ forbade paying taxes to Caesar (Luke 23:2)
54. Treated with contempt by Herod and his soldiers; mocked and then returned to Pilate (Luke 23:11)

55. Chosen over a convicted robber, Barabbas, to be killed (Matt. 27:20)
56. He was whipped, scourged (Matt. 27:26)
57. Religious leaders vehemently accused Him before Herod (Luke 23:10)
58. He was delivered to be crucified (Matt. 27:26)
59. He was stripped (Matt. 27:28)
60. Then enrobed in scarlet in mockery (Matt. 27:28)
61. Crown of thorns mashed upon His forehead (Matt. 27:29)
62. His beard was plucked (Isa. 50:6)
63. In mockery a reed was put in His hand for a scepter (Matt. 27:29)
64. In derision they bowed before Him (Matt. 27:29)
65. Once again they spat on Him (Matt. 27:30; 26:67)
66. Removing the reed from His hand, they beat Him with it (Matt. 27:30)
67. The crowd, chief priests, scribes, elders and robbers all ridiculed Him (Matt. 27:31)
68. The robe was taken off Him (Matt. 27:31; Ps. 22:18)
69. He bore His own cross for a while (Matt. 27:32)
70. He was crucified (Matt 27:35; Psa. 22:16b)
71. In shame and ignominy, disgraced between two robbers (Matt. 27:38; Isa. 53:9)
72. Wagging their heads, passersby reviled Him (Matt. 27:39)
73. He died (Matt. 27:50)

WHO JESUS CHRIST IS

To the Architect He is the Chief Cornerstone
To the Artist He is the One Altogether Lovely
To the Astronomer He is the Sun of Righteousness
To the Author He is Source of the Book of Books
To the Baker He is the Living Bread of Life
To the Banker He is the Hidden Treasure
To the Builder He is the Sure and Only Foundation
To the Carpenter He is the Door
To the Diplomat He is the Desire of All Nations
To the Doctor He is the Great Physician
To the Editor He is the Good News
To the Educator He is a Teacher come from God
To the Electrician He is the Light of the World
To the Farmer He is the Lord of the Harvest
To the Florist He is the Lily of the Valley, the Rose of Sharon
To the Fraternalist He is the Blessed and Only Potentate
To the Geologist He is the Rock of Ages
To the Geriatrician He is the Ancient of Days
To the Historian He is the Author of His Story
To the Industrialist He is the Chief Executive Officer
To the Jeweler He is the Owner of the Pearl of Great Price
To the Juror He is the Faithful and True Witness
To the King He is the Power behind the throne
To the Laborer He is the Giver of Rest

To the Lawyer He is the Advocate with God the Father
To the Magistrate He is the Righteous Judge
To the Navigator He is the Bright, Morning Star
To the Olympian He is the Forerunner
To the Pastor He is the Head of the Church
To the Pawn Shop Owner He is the Redeemer
To the Pharmacist He is a Balm in Gilead
To the Philosopher He is the Wisdom of God
To the Politician He is King of kings and Lord of lords
To the Preacher He is the Word of God
To the Psychiatrist He is the Counselor
To the Publisher He is Author of the world's Best Seller
To the Quizmaster He is the Answer to every question
To the Referee He is the Final Decision
To the Sailor He is the Anchor of Hope
To the Sculptor He is the Living Stone
To the Servant He is the Good Master
To the Sinner He is the Lamb of God who takes away sin
To the Slave He is the Liberator whose Truth sets free
To the Soldier He is our Peace
To the Theologian He is the Author and Finisher of our Faith
To the Undertaker He is the Conqueror of Death
To the Union Representative He is the Only Mediator
        between God and man

CHRIST IN ALL THE SCRIPTURES

Genesis—Seed of the woman—3:15
Exodus—Passover Lamb of God—12
Leviticus—Atoning Sacrifice—17
Numbers—Smitten Rock—20:8,11
Deuteronomy—Prophet like unto Moses—18:15, 18
Joshua—Captain of the Lord's Host—5:15
Judges—Divine Deliverer—2:18
Ruth—Kinsman Redeemer—3:12
1 Samuel—Anointed One Rejected—2:10
2 Samuel—Son of David—7:14
1 & 2 Kings—Glorious Coming King
1 & 2 Chronicles—Vigilant Administrator
Ezra—Wise Leader—6:14–15
Nehemiah—Prayerful Builder
Esther—Prevailing Intercessor—4:14, 16
Job—Living Redeemer—19:25
Psalms—Praise of Israel—150:6
Proverbs—Wisdom of God—8:22–23
Ecclesiastes—Great Teacher
Song of Solomon—My Beloved—5:10
Isaiah—Suffering Servant—53:11
Jeremiah—Weeping Prophet—9:1
Lamentation—Man of Sorrows
Ezekiel—God of Glory Enthroned
Daniel—Ancient of Days, Smiting Stone
Hosea—Lover of the Unfaithful—3:1

Joel—Hope of Israel—3:16
Amos—Rescuer of Israel—3:12
Obadiah—Deliverer upon Mt. Zion—verse 17
Jonah—Resurrected One—2:10
Micah—Everlasting God—5:2
Nahum—Stronghold—1:7
Habakkuk—Holy God—1:13
Zephaniah—King of Israel—3:15
Haggai—Desire of All Nations—2:7
Zechariah—Righteous Branch—3:8
Malachi—Sun of Righteousness—4:2

Matthew—King of the Jews—2:2
Mark—Servant of the Lord—10:45
Luke—Son of Man—19:10
John—Son of God—1:1
Acts—Ascended Lord—1:9–10
Romans—Our Righteousness—1:17
1 Corinthians—Conqueror of Death—15:20
2 Corinthians—Our Sufficiency—12:9
Galatians—Liberator—5:1
Ephesians—Exalted Head of the Church—1:22
Philippians—Our Joy—1:26
Colossians—Fullness of Deity—2:9
1 Thessalonians—Our Comfort—4:16–17
2 Thessalonians—Our Glory—1:12
1 Timothy—Mediator—2:5
2 Timothy—Our Rewarder—4:8

Titus—Our Blessed Hope—2:13
Philemon—Our Substitute—verse 17
Hebrews—High Priest—4:15
James—Lord of Sabaoth (Hosts)—5:4
1 Peter—Shepherd and Bishop of our Souls—2:25
2 Peter—Morning Star—1:19
1 John—Word of Life—1:1
2 John—Our Truth—verses 1–2
3 John—Truth Personified—verses 3–4
Jude—Believers' Security—verses 24–25
Revelation—Alpha and Omega—1:8

Church

CHURCH ANNIVERSARIES

One of the things I occasionally do when preaching a church anniversary sermon is to list the great historical events in the United States (or world) through which the church has lived. The latest World Almanac is useful here and should be a part of every pastor's library. Include also those local events which had an impact upon the church. Begin with the year the church was founded, and emphasize the fact that through it all, God in Christ kept the church.

Slavery; Emancipation; organization of the Ku Klux Klan (1866); end of the Reconstruction era (1877); founding of the Tuskegee Institute (1881); Spanish-American War (1898); lynchings and Jim Crow; the first successful plane flight (1903); founding of the NAACP (1909). The influenza epidemic that killed 548,000 in the U.S.; the end of World War I (1918); Prohibition (1919); Depression (1929).

World War II (1941); dropping of the first atomic bomb (1945); Korean conflict (1950); public school segregation ruled unconstitutional (1954); Montgomery, Alabama bus boycott (1955); civil rights sit-ins (1960); march to Washington, D.C. (1963); Vietnam War (1964); Martin Luther King, Jr., assassinated (1968); lunar landing (1969); Watergate (1972); U.S. Centennial (1976).

Hostages in Iran (1979); first permanent artificial heart transplant (1982); Apartheid defeated (1990); Kuwait invaded by Iraq (1991); O.J. Simpson acquitted of murder; 169 killed in Oklahoma City bombing; "Million Man March" (1995); Septuplets born to Iowa woman (1997); President Clinton's impeachment trial (1999); etc.

Through it all—hurricanes, floods, droughts, volcanic eruptions, earthquakes, race riots, disastrous strikes, hijackings, plane crashes, etc.—the Lord has kept His church. And He will preserve it until the Rapture!

CHURCH ANNIVERSARY: SERMON TEXTS

1 Chron. 12:38: Serving the King

Ps. 84:1: A Lovely Dwelling Place

Ps. 100: How to Enter God's Presence:
  With Gladness, Well-Grounded, With Gratitude

Ps. 111:1: Praise in the Assembly

Ps. 122:1: A Delightful Invitation

Isa. 28:16; 1 Pet. 2:6–8: The Chief Cornerstone

Matt. 16:18: The Victorious Church

John 20:19–25: The Excitement of Going to Church
  (F.W. Dixon)

Acts 2:41–47: The Inner Life of the Church
  (F.W. Dixon)

Acts 10:31: The Ideal Church (F.W. Dixon)

Acts 20:28: Purchased, Precious, Purpose
1 Cor. 3:11; Matt. 16:18; 1 Tim. 3:15: A Firm Foundation:
    Its Base, Its Builder, Its Backbone (pillar and ground)
1 Cor. 6:11: The Such-Were-Some-of-You Baptist Church
1 Cor. 7:23 (6:20): Bought with a Price
Eph. 5:25: Christ, a Gift for the Church
1 Tim. 3:15: What the Church Is
1 Pet. 2:9: Called Out to Lift Up!

CHURCH BUSINESS MEETINGS

Baptists should not view local church autonomy as license for violating the Scriptures which teach all things are to be done decently and in order (1 Cor. 14:40). Too often church members see the "business" aspect of the meeting as being secular and not spiritual. Actually the church business meeting is a part of our worship of God. The fact the meeting may not be held in the main auditorium or sanctuary does not preclude the concept of worship.

Since the pastor is usually the moderator of the meeting, he should see to it, with the help of the deacons, that a worshipful attitude or atmosphere is maintained. When made the object of prayer rather than power plays, the church meeting can bring glory to Christ. Patience, honesty, courtesy and kindness should be manifested and love made the all-pervading characteristic.

There are pastors who dislike church meetings and seek to have as few of them as possible, sometimes even in violation of their constitution and bylaws. It is true we are in the Laodicean church age (Rev. 3:14), and the trend against authority is predicted to increase. But the pastor who prays, obeys the bylaws, seeks to teach his people the Word of God and keeps under Holy Spirit control the wielding of authority, will help his congregation come to see the church business meeting as an opportunity to exalt the Lord Jesus Christ.

Sample Agenda of a Business Meeting:

I. Call to Order
II. Devotional Exercise
    A. Hymn
    B. Scriptures
    C. Prayer
    D. Share Time (testimonies, hymns, etc.)
III. After ascertaining quorum, motion to proceed, then adoption of Agenda.
IV. Reading and Acceptance of Minutes of Previous Meeting
V. Unfinished Business
    A. Items from minutes
    B. Reports
        1. Committees, if any
        2. Church School
        3. Church auxiliaries or clubs
        4. Financial
        5. Deacons
        6. Pastoral
        7. Other
        8. Calendar

VI. New Business; announcements
VII. Motion to Adjourn; closing prayer.

THE CHARACTER OF A CHURCH

Each church or local assembly has its own distinct character. It is a complex personality, one determined by many factors. Without attempting to assign weights or values, consider the following components which help establish the character or personality of a church and make it distinctive:

1. ADMINISTRATIVE: Constitution and Bylaws; Date and time for Communion, Baptism. Special Days observed, like Anniversaries, etc. Working Staff: caretaker, secretaries, etc. Attendance: Sunday mornings, evenings; Bible Class; Prayer meeting; etc.
2. AFFILIATIONS: National and State conventions, local conferences and associations.
3. BOARDS AND AUXILIARIES: Deacons and Trustees: numbers, ages, strengths, weaknesses, skills, training, Benevolence Fund qualifications, etc. Joint Boards; Mothers; Clubs and Auxiliaries: How many? Purposes? Leadership?
4. BUILDING, PROPERTY: Location: part of city or town, main thoroughfares, changing neighborhood, etc. Type of building: age, size, architecture, heating system, storefront, parking lot, value of property, etc.

5. FINANCES: Debt? Amount, kind (mortgage, loan); methods of raising money: tithing, programs, etc. Amount in treasury; Income: weekly, monthly, quarterly, annually; insurances, salaries, etc.

6. HISTORY: Age of church: when founded. Conflicts and litigation; reputation in community; overall spiritual tone; emphasis on Evangelism, Missions, Christian Education.

7. MEMBERSHIP: Education, economic status, birthplaces, ages, demography; founding families still present? Male-Female: role of women in the church. Marital status: married, single, divorced, separated, widowed. Number of children.

8. MUSIC: Musicians: number, training. Music: gospel, hymns, cantatas, anthems, spirituals. Number of singing groups: choirs, choruses, ensembles, etc. Instruments: piano, organ; their condition, brand, model.

9. PASTORAL: Number of pastors; lengths of pastorates; founding pastor still serving? Emeritus? Age(s) of previous pastors and present minister. Associate ministers: ages, training, goals, duties.

10. SUNDAY SCHOOL: Organization, trained teachers, size of school, classrooms, equipment, attendance, Vacation Bible School, etc.

Obviously, by the time you consider these factors for any one given local church, it is easy to see the many differences that give each assembly its distinctiveness, individuality or uniqueness.

I think that I shall never see
A church that's all it ought to be;
A church whose members never stray
Beyond the straight and narrow way;
A church that has no empty pews,
Whose pastor never has the blues;
A church whose deacons always "deak"
And none is proud, and all are meek;
Where gossips never peddle lies,
Or make complaints or criticize;
Where all are always sweet and kind,
To all of others' faults are blind.
Such perfect churches there may be,
But none of them is known to me.
But still, we'll work, and pray and plan
To make our own the best we can.

THE CHURCH COVENANT

Having been led, as we believe, by the Spirit of God to receive the Lord Jesus Christ as our Savior, and on the profession of our faith having been baptized in the name of the Father, and of the Son, and of the Holy Spirit, we do now, in the presence of God and angels, most solemnly and joyfully enter into covenant with one another, as one body in Christ.

We engage, therefore, by the aid of the Holy Spirit, to walk together in Christian love;

To strive for the advancement of this church in knowledge,

holiness and comfort;

To promote its prosperity and spirituality;

To sustain its worship, ordinances, discipline and doctrines;

To give it a sacred preeminence over all institutions of human origin;

To contribute cheerfully and regularly to the support of the ministry, the expenses of the church, the relief of the poor and the spread of the gospel through all nations.

We also engage to maintain family and secret devotion;

To religiously educate our children;

To seek the salvation of our kindred and acquaintances;

To walk circumspectly in the world;

To be just in our dealings, faithful in our engagements, and exemplary in our deportment;

To avoid all tattling, backbiting and excessive anger;

To abstain from the sale and use of intoxicating drinks as a beverage, and to be zealous in our efforts to advance the kingdom of our Savior.

We further engage to watch over one another in brotherly love;

To remember each other in prayer;

To aid each other in sickness and distress;

To cultivate Christian sympathy in feeling and courtesy in speech;

To be slow to take offense but always ready for reconciliation, and mindful of the rules of our Savior, to secure it without delay.

We moreover engage, that when we remove from this place,

we will as soon as possible unite with some other church where we can carry out the spirit of this covenant and the principles of God's Word.

CHURCH DISCIPLINE

The last church age is the Laodicean (Rev. 3:14–19), which literally means the people rule, express their "rights." As such an age grows, it becomes increasingly difficult to administer discipline in the local assembly. That there should be discipline, however, is plainly taught by the Bible. When discipline is neglected, the testimony of the church is vitiated, her witness weakened, respect for those in God-given positions of authority and esteem is lessened, and the Head of the Church is grieved.

Christians are obligated to keep their churches morally clean. We have the responsibility to teach, to provide good instruction from the Bible, the Word of God, which calls for correction, rebuke, chastisement and even removal from the fellowship (1 Cor. 5:6–13). Some church members contend that no one should ever be put out of the church. But the authority for church discipline is the Bible. And because a little leaven leavens the whole lump, the church should not be hesitant to administer discipline that includes "disfellowshipping." Discipline is good for the church.

Fellowship should be withdrawn from: (1) Those members who refuse to settle their personal differences (Matt. 18:15–17); (2) the known ("commonly reported") sinner (1 Cor. 5:9–11); (3) the member who refuses to work for a living (2 Thess. 3:6–15);

(4) the member who deliberately causes divisions, schisms within the local assembly (Tit. 3:10–11; Rom. 16:17). Where the offender repents and confesses, the church in love is to forgive and restore (2 Cor. 2:5–11).

But the pastor must be careful to remember we live in a litigious age, one given to going to court (sue-sappy saints). Therefore make sure the proper steps are taken in the procedure used to withdraw fellowship from an offender. Follow the steps outlined in the Church's Constitution and Bylaws, or see the general principles offered in *The Hiscox Guide for Baptist Churches.* It is especially important that the one tried by the church be informed of the nature of the charge(s) and be given adequate opportunity to vindicate himself (herself). A new pastor may find himself in a church sorely lacking discipline. In such a situation it may be necessary for him to seek to bring the people to the point where the whole church supports a plan for discipline. This will require much prayer, plain Bible teaching and preaching (2 Tim. 3:16–4:2). It is indeed the responsibility of the church to teach God's standards (1 Tim. 3:15) for church behavior.

When the apostle dealt with the problem in the church in Corinth—immorality and the "puffed-up" refusal of the church to deal with the wayward members—he gave at least three reasons the church should administer discipline. First, for the good of the offender; second, for the good of the assembly; and third, for the good of the world. My outline is: Culprit (1 Cor. 5:1–5), Church (vv. 6–8), Cosmos (vv. 9–13).

Discipline really is an expression of love calculated to reclaim the sinner (Gal. 6:1–5) by moving him to repentance; to strengthen the local assembly; to give a proper witness to the world. So the pastor must not be hasty and thoughtless here. Church discipline cannot be properly enforced by him alone or by a few people. Time is required to get rid of carnality and worldliness which deter discipline. Once the church as a whole adopts a plan for discipline, and it is clearly announced, there should be no hesitation in enforcing it.

One of the common problems we have concerns unwed mothers. A policy must be established to deal with members who commit fornication and it becomes publicly evident. To allow them to remain in membership without anything being said or done is to do great harm. An unrepentant, unwed mother allowed to remain in the church has a bad influence upon the other young ladies in the congregation.

Only God gives life, so we do not speak against innocent babies. But unwed parents handicap the child. And the fact that children are a gift of God does not absolve members who commit fornication (1 Cor. 6:18) or adultery. An unwed mother, by virtue of her pregnancy and birth of a child, makes a public statement of a private sin. If she is to remain in fellowship she must make a public confession and repentance. The rule to keep in mind: **Private sin calls for private confession; public sin demands public confession.**

Furthermore, if a man who is a member of the church is known to be the father of the child born out of wedlock, he should face the same discipline. Usually in such cases spiritually-minded deaconesses are sent to speak with the unwed mother. It may be the policy of the church for the deacons and pastor to handle the matter or for both groups to become involved.

The member is encouraged to come to prayer meeting or evening service to publicly confess and ask forgiveness, and the membership then present entertains the recommendation made by the Deacon Board. This action is then simply announced at the next church business meeting.

TRADITIONAL CHURCHES

Young Black ministers are being taught in certain circles to abandon the idea of pastoring old, already established churches— "traditional churches"—in favor of starting new works. The success in terms of membership numbers and attendance enjoyed by those who have founded works is heady and seems to point to the wisdom of not pastoring traditional Black churches. By the same token, not all newly founded assemblies have prospered numerically; some have failed and folded up.

We would argue that no minister should attempt to slam the door in the face of the Holy Spirit. It is a highly individualistic matter, and each preacher will have to be led by the Spirit of God. Caution is advised for those who think founding new assemblies is the only route for the young Black minister to take. With all of their faults, there is still to be found in many so-called traditional churches a warmth and camaraderie, a courtesy, a sophistication and an appreciation of history and the struggle through which the grace of God has brought them.

And after all, God has produced throughout the years of Black Church history many capable, God-fearing ministers, missionaries, musicians and Christian workers. It may appear ludicrous then for one who was saved in a traditional church, or whose parents were saved in a traditional church, now to refuse to accept a pastorate in a traditional church! God has His people in such assemblies; they are sheep in need of a shepherd. And while it may be quite a struggle to break through—to get rid of liberal Sunday School literature, to encourage Bible reading, prayer meeting attendance, Bible class attendance, etc.—the enabling power of the Holy Spirit is available.

To close the door on traditional Black churches may produce a separatist attitude that is "holier than thou" (Isa. 65:5) and lead to a failure to have fellowship with those ministers of traditional churches who believe in the shed blood of Jesus Christ. If one's purpose is to escape corruption, discipline problems, etc., only time will tell whether the new church escapes. More than likely, after ten or fifteen years, the new churches will face problems similar to those of the traditional churches, but lacking the sophistication and spirituality may find themselves unable to adequately cope.

My advice to the young Black minister: Don't automatically close the door on the traditional church. It is not inconceivable that the Lord still calls men into the pastorates of such assemblies. And it is a challenging option!

WATCHCARE

"Watchcare" is the word used to describe the membership of the person who desires a church home while away from home, without severing relations with his or her home church. It is a provision made for those believers of like faith who reside temporarily in a city—a college student, a person working a temporary job, etc. As watchcare members, they do not vote and are not allowed to hold elective office but otherwise enjoy all the other privileges of membership. Some churches include the right to vote at Business Meetings; others limit the right to vote to matters which do not determine or have an impact upon the Church's Convention affiliation. There are churches which make no provision for this category of membership.

It is claimed by those who oppose the concept that the practice has obfuscated the perception of what true church membership really is. However, one should not blame "sporadic non-committed" membership attitudes upon watchcare. Watchcare members are not necessarily irresponsible nor does the idea of watchcare create irresponsibility. Actually, believers who go through the process of becoming watchcare members show an initiative that should be appreciated. After all, multitudes who leave our churches and relocate (1) stop attending church altogether or go spasmodically; (2) attend different churches when they do go; (3) attend the same church whenever they go but do not join.

The argument that the early church did not practice watchcare ignores the basic reason for watchcare in these days of heightened mobility. There were no automobiles and modes of rapid transportation in Bible days; no mass job displacements, factory shut downs and relocations; better job offers; opportunities to attend colleges and universities. Finally, in answer to the objection that watchcare is detrimental to church stability and membership accountability, it is noted that some churches terminate the watchcare status after six (6) months, at which time the person must signify his or her intentions to become a regular member. Failure to follow this procedure may indicate a lack of interest, and membership is terminated by the church.

Communion

GENERAL

Fermented wine is not the proper element to use to represent the uncorrupted blood of the Lord Jesus Christ. Just as unleavened bread is used to represent His sinless body, so the "fruit of the vine" should not be fermented. In fact, it is interesting that the word "wine" is not used in the New Testament with respect to the Lord's Supper. Rather, the words "cup" and "fruit of the vine" are used (Matt. 26:27–29; Mark 14:23–25; Luke 22:17–20; 1 Cor. 11:25–28).

A study of the Hebrew and Greek words translated "wine" reveals wine may be fresh-pressed juice or fermented. But leaven, a type of sin, is forbidden by the Torah during the days of the Passover. Leading rabbis extended the command to include its presence in wine as well as in bread. We believe fermented wine is an improper symbol. The body of the Lord Jesus saw no corruption (Ps. 16:10; Acts 2:27; 13:35).

His body did not decompose or rot because His blood was the result of supernatural conception. Since none of the blood of the mother flows to the fetus and the Lord Jesus had no human father, His blood was sinless, divine, innocent, incorruptible, cleansing. Therefore fermented wine should not be used to represent that blood.

Another thing commonly found in our churches is the misunderstanding of the word "unworthily" in 1 Corinthians 11:27, 29. This adverb modifies the verbs "eat" and "drink," thus referring to the manner in which we partake of the Supper. Emphasis is upon conduct, not upon character. If it were "unworthy" instead of "unworthily," it would refer to the character of the participant. Pastors then must warn members not to partake of Communion with levity, gum-chewing, glibness, flippancy, indifference, carelessness or irreverence. We are to recognize its solemnity, appreciate its meaning and then partake. Failure here may lead to physical weakness, illness and death.

Different churches serve the Supper at different times. The words "as often as you eat this bread, and drink this cup" set no specific time schedule or frequency. Most Baptists celebrate the Lord's Supper once a month, although on varying Sundays. This is to say, one church will serve on the first Sunday, another church on the third Sunday, etc. And there are churches which observe Communion in connection with a regular morning service, while others have a separate afternoon service. Still others, who believe that "supper" should be served in the evening, observe Communion therefore in the evening.

A separate service is commended by some pastors because there is more participation in the testimony period. Having to make a special effort to return may indeed bring spiritual blessings. Finally, note that in the actual serving of the elements a great variety of methods are used. Some churches make one prayer for both elements; others eat as the elements are distributed. For them "together" does not mean all at the same time. Other assemblies wait until all are served the bread, then eat; or all are served the cup, then drink. Some serve both bread and cup, then eat and drink.

Use of a single, common cup is frowned upon for hygienic reasons. Then in some assemblies the members leave their seats to obtain the elements. In most Black Baptist churches the deacons serve the people seated in the pews. The new pastor should observe the tradition of the established church and broadmindedly recognize there is much variety in methods of worship in the Communion service.

EXAMPLE: ORDER OF COMMUNION SERVICE

1. Testimony Period: Deacons are in charge as members sing, pray and testify. If this is a separate service, the officers at this point may lift the Regular Offering first and then the Benevolent Fund Offering.
2. Right Hand of Fellowship for New Members. Those joining the church may be given a copy of the Church Covenant, Baptism certificate, envelopes, membership card, a copy of the Constitution/Bylaws, etc., at this time.
3. Read the Church Covenant responsively.
4. Communion Talk or Scripture Reading by the Pastor.
5. Prayer, by the pastor or by a designated deacon, and Distribution of the Bread by the deacons. Partake in unison.
6. Prayer, by the pastor or by a designated deacon, and Distribution of the Cup by the deacons. Partake in unison.

7. Benediction: "And when they had sung a hymn, they went out to the mount of Olives" (Matt. 26:30; Mark 14:26). May close with "When We All Get to Heaven," or "Climbing Jacob's Ladder," or "Face to Face," etc.

SCRIPTURES: TO BE READ AT THE LORD'S TABLE

"He has the Word that spake it,
He took the bread and brake it;
And what that Word did make it,
I do believe and take it."—*John Donne*

Isa. 53:3–6: He is despised and rejected by men, a Man of sorrows and acquainted with grief. And we hid, as it were, our faces from Him; He was despised, and we did not esteem Him. Surely He has borne our griefs and carried our sorrows; yet we esteemed Him stricken, smitten by God, and afflicted. But He was wounded for our transgressions, He was bruised for our iniquities; the chastisement for our peace was upon Him, and by His stripes we are healed. All we like sheep have gone astray; we have turned, every one, to his own way; and the Lord has laid on Him the iniquity of us all.

Matt. 26:17–30: Now on the first day of the Feast of the Un-leavened Bread the disciples came to Jesus, saying to Him, "Where do You want us to prepare for You to eat the Pass-over?" And He said, "Go into the city to a certain man, and say to him, 'The Teacher says, "My time is at hand; I will keep the Passover at your house with My Disciples."'" So the disciples did as Jesus had directed them; and they prepared the Passover. When evening had come, He sat down with the twelve. Now as they were eating, He said, "Assuredly, I say to you, one of you will betray Me." And they were exceedingly sorrowful, and each of them began to say to Him, "Lord, is it I?" Then He answered and said, "He who dipped his hand with Me in the dish will betray Me. The Son of Man goes just as it is written of Him, but woe to that man by whom the Son of Man is betrayed! It would have been good for that man if he had not been born." Then Judas, who was betraying Him, answered and said, "Rabbi, is it I?" He said to him, "You have said it." And as they were eating, Jesus took bread, blessed it and broke it, and gave it to the disciples and said, "Take, eat; this is My body." Then He took the cup, and gave thanks, and gave it to them, saying, "Drink from it, all of you. For this is My blood of the new covenant, which is shed for many for the remission of sins. But I say to you, I will not drink of this fruit of the vine from now on until that day when I drink it new with you in My Father's kingdom." And when they had sung a hymn, they went out to the Mount of Olives.

Mark 14:22–25: And as they were eating, Jesus took bread, blessed and broke it, and gave it to them and said, "Take, eat; this is My body." Then He took the cup, and when He had given thanks He gave it to them, and they all drank from it. And He said to them, "This is My blood of the new covenant, which is shed for many. Assuredly, I say to you, I will no longer drink of the fruit of the vine until that day when I drink it new in the kingdom of God."

Luke 22:14–20: When the hour had come, He sat down, and the twelve apostles with Him. Then He said to them, "With fervent desire I have desired to eat this Passover with you before I suffer; for I say to you, I will no longer eat of it until it is fulfilled in the kingdom of God." Then He took the cup, and gave thanks, and said, "Take this and divide it among yourselves; for I say to you, I will not drink of the fruit of the vine until the kingdom of God comes." And He took bread, gave thanks and broke it, and gave it to them saying, "This is My body which is given for you; do this in remembrance of Me." Likewise He also took the cup after supper, saying, "This cup is the new covenant in My blood, which is shed for you."

1 Cor. 10:16–17: The cup of blessing which we bless, is it not the communion of the blood of Christ? The bread which we break, is it not the communion of the body of Christ? For we, though many, are one bread and one body; for we all partake of that one bread.

1 Cor. 11:23–32: For I received from the Lord that which I also delivered to you: that the Lord Jesus on the same night in which He was betrayed took bread; and when He had given thanks, He broke it and said, "Take, eat; this is My body which is broken for you; do this in remembrance of Me." In the same manner He also took the cup after supper, saying, "This cup is the new covenant in My blood. This do, as often as you drink it, in remembrance of Me."

For as often as you eat this bread and drink this cup, you proclaim the Lord's death till He comes. Therefore whoever eats this bread or drinks this cup of the Lord in an unworthy manner will be guilty of the body and blood of the Lord. But let a man examine himself, and so let him eat of the bread and drink of the cup. For he who eats and drinks in an unworthy manner eats and drinks judgment to himself, not discerning the Lord's body. For this reason many are weak and sick among you, and many sleep. For if we would judge ourselves, we would not be judged. But when we are judged, we are chastened by the Lord, that we may not be condemned with the world.

TOPICS FOR TALKS

Gen. 18:1–8: Heavenly Hospitality

Ps. 23:5: God's Table

Matt. 26:26: The Lord's Body

Matt. 26:28: Remission of Sins

Matt. 26:29: My Father's Kingdom (A Foretaste of Heaven)

Mark 14:23: Thanksgiving in Communion

Mark 14:24: A New Covenant

Luke 22:19: Memorials—In Remembrance of Me

John 6:35: The Bread of Life

John 6:53–56: Belief: Assimilation

Rom. 6:3–4: Buried in Baptism

Rom. 6:4: Beginning a New Relationship

1 Cor. 10:16–17: Bread-Breaking Brotherhood

1 Cor. 11:23: The Same Night

The Art of Remembrance: The Sabbath: Exod. 20:8; Col. 2:16–17; The Slave: Deut. 15:15; The Creator: Eccl. 12:1; Lot's Wife: Luke 17:32; The Savior: 1 Cor. 11:24–25

1 Cor. 11:26: Coming Again—Till He Comes

1 Cor. 12:27: The Body of Christ

Eph. 4:4–6: The Oneness of It All

Phil. 2:5–8: Humility, a Basis for Communion

Phil. 3:10: The Fellowship of His Sufferings (The Cup)

Col. 3:16: Singing After Supper (Matt 26:30)

Rev. 3:20: An Invitation to Supper

Rev. 19:6–9: Called to the Marriage Supper

Counseling

The pulpit ministry is an excellent forum for counseling, and the pastor who teaches his congregation often eliminates the necessity for private counseling. However, pastors are cautioned not to seek to make their churches mere counseling centers. There are other Christian agencies which specialize in family counseling and, with trained workers, can be more than helpful. Preachers who concentrate their ministry on building up the Black family must be careful lest they think they have discovered the key to successful church building.

Such counseling, of course, is needed—but not at the expense of failing to maintain a well-rounded ministry, one that is not blind to the fact that there are other important aspects of the Bible that need to be taught and preached. Pastors must provide balanced meals for the sheep if they are to grow into Christlikeness. This is really the main point we are driving at: preaching (teaching) that is balanced.

The menu must not always offer messages on family life or marriage (or for that matter on stewardship, or baptism, etc.). There is not only the peril of the pastor creating a lopsided ministry, but there is the danger of becoming emotionally and physically involved with the one counseled. Immorality ever lurks at the door! Be careful!

Daffinitions
By Banks

Choose the correct answer

1. Abel:
    a. an object to be rung
    b. capable
    c. a son of Adam

2. Amos:
    a. an O.T. prophet
    b. a necessity
    c. Andy's partner

3. Apostle:
    a. a package
    b. one commissioned
    c. the husband of an epistle

4. Baal:
    a. bond
    b. what we do to cotton
    c. idol god

5. Beersheba:
    a. Dan's wife
    b. Bathsheba's sister
    c. a town in Edom

6. Bishop:
    a. an elder
    b. comedian Joey
    c. a place where people buy things

7. Caesar:
    a. Roman emperor
    b. a sudden attack, fit
    c. a command: grab her!

8. Cain:
    a. the first murderer
    b. what some people raise
    c. a source of sugar

9. Covenant:
    a. an agreement
    b. fit, suitable
    c. an insect that lives in a cove

10. Epistle: a. a gun
                    b. wife of an apostle
                    c. a letter

11. Exile: a. captivity
                  b. outside of an isle
                  c. pin on which a wheel revolves

12. Greece: a. shortening
                  b. European country
                  c. lubrication

13. Israel: a. no sham
                  b. Jewish nation
                  c. inquiry about Ray's health

14. Job: a. an O.T. character
                  b. work
                  c. Roman god

15. Jude: a. sack fiber
                  b. haggled
                  c. a N.T. letter

16. Remnant: a. left-over
                  b. a N.T. letter
                  c. a famous artist

17. Rome: a. short for Jerome
                  b. city in Italy
                  c. wander, go astray

18. Satan: a. glossy, silk fabric
                  b. Devil
                  c. past tense for sit-in

19. Sodom: a. Edom's cousin
                  b. Gomorrah's brother
                  c. very stupid
                  d. wicked city

20. Tittle: a. a pro-football star
                  b. the first cousin of jot
                  c. part of a letter of the Hebrew alphabet

Deacons
1 Timothy 3:8–13

The word "deacon" (*diakonos*) means servant, waiter, aide; it does not mean "ruler." Every pastor should know this and seek to maintain the scriptural significance of the office of deacon. Furthermore, the idea of a "trial" or "walking" deacon is not Biblical. The man chosen to become a deacon is to prove by the life he lives *before* he is chosen that he is a satisfactory candidate for the office. Note in Acts 6:3, that the apostles appointed the men to serve (*diakonein*) after the congregation had helped to select them:

"Therefore, brethren, seek out from among you seven men of good reputation, full of the Holy Spirit and wisdom, whom we may appoint (*kathistemi*: set down, place, put down) over this business." This indicates pastors should supervise the work of the deacons.

In short, spiritual leaders are to lay down the guidelines; the church selects potential deacons according to these guidelines, and the spiritual leaders then make appointments from this list chosen by the church. Deacons are not elected deacons for life. It is not automatic that once a deacon, always a deacon. Neither is the office transferable.

A man who is a deacon in one church and leaves to join another church is not automatically a deacon in the new church.

Wisdom dictates that deacons be elected for a stated limited time, preferably one year, and then annually as they are needed— and with the right to serve as long as they are elected each year. This, of course, may end up being a life-time appointment, but still the church should make the decision every year.

What about divorced men serving as deacons? See the section on Divorce and Remarriage. There are those who interpret "the husband of one wife" to mean: (1) not polygamous, (2) a one-wife kind of a man. I would agree with John L. Rice who stated that a divorced man who lives a good clean Christian life, who has proven himself, has sought God's forgiveness, ought not be forbidden to serve if God has called him to serve. "If he is the most spiritual and useful and godly man for the place, then he probably ought to be selected and ought to be used" (*Here Is My Question*, p. 134, Dr. John L. Rice, Sword of the Lord Publishers, Murfreesboro, Tenn, 1962).

The Death of Infants
Babies In Heaven

What about babies in Heaven? I cannot answer who, what, why, where or when with respect to the status of babies who die. However let me share with you some thoughts and some questions. Dr. Donald G. Barnhouse was of the opinion that the millions of babies in so-called non-Christian lands who die, go to be with the Lord. He suggested this is God's way of balancing out, so to speak, the numbers with those who live in countries where the gospel *is* preached. This is an attempt in part to satisfy those who ask, "Is it fair to condemn to Hell those who have never heard the gospel?" (Actually, condemnation is not because they have not heard but because they are sinners.)

Will there be any babies in Heaven? Or will they all be adults when we get there? Indeed, what will *you* look like in Heaven? Will you appear then as you looked when you were 33 years old, based upon the belief that the Lord Jesus was 33 when He died? Of course it is believed we will know our loved ones in Heaven. When the son of David and Bathsheba died (2 Sam. 12:14–23), David said, "I shall go to him, but he shall not return to me." It is also interesting that somehow Simon Peter recognized Moses and Elijah there on the Mount of Transfiguration (Matt. 17:3–4). And in Luke 16:23, the rich man in hell recognized Lazarus and Abraham when he saw them together in Paradise.

Theologians often speak of an age of accountability. At what age is a child held accountable by God as a sinner because he is conscious of his sin? It probably varies, although I am tempted to suggest that these modern days—principally because of television—have caused the age to be lower than it was a generation ago. The old nature, of course, is still in all of us. But many Christian scholars believe that the sin nature of an unaccountable infant is paid for by the blood of Christ.

Some Bible teachers add that this is because (1) all shall be made alive (1 Cor. 15:22), all in the graves shall hear His voice, even those who die as infants (John 5:25–29); (2) God is longsuffering toward us, not willing that any should perish (2 Pet. 3:9). So little ones, not accountable, not known as intentional rebellious sinners against God, are believed to be taken to heaven (Dr. John Rice).

Dedication of Infants

This basic procedure of dedication is usually incorporated in the morning service:

1. Call by name the parents, the child, the godparents.
2. State to the congregation the policy of the church, since infants are not baptized.
3. Read a portion of any one (or more) of the following scriptures: 1 Sam. 1:20–28; Ps. 103:17–18; Prov. 22:6; Matt. 18:10,14; Matt. 19:13–15 (Mark 10:13–16; Luke 18:15–17); Luke 2:21, 25–30, 33, 40.
4. Seek to impress upon the parents their God-given responsibility to pray for the child and so live before it that God will honor their desire for the infant to grow up and be saved. Commend the godparents as well.
5. Place your hand gently upon the child (some ministers take the child up into their arms), and pray the prayer of dedication.
6. Give the parents a certificate of Infant Dedication.

> This child we dedicate to Thee
> O God of grace and purity.
> In Thy great love its life prolong,
> Shield it, we pray, from sin and wrong.
> —*Author unknown*

Devotions: Personal
"Take heed to yourself." 1 Tim. 4:16

It is absolutely essential that the Pastor spend time each morning in personal devotions. Preachers who are always preaching and teaching, but who seldom study, pray and have devotions, get into spiritual trouble. There is no better way to start the day than to read a devotional message, meditate upon the verse selected and then spend time in prayer.

Devotional books have been the major source of sermon seeds for me throughout my pastoral ministry. If you are not already in the habit of having your own private devotions each morning, start now! You will never regret it.

Definitions of the D.D. Degree

1. Dumb Dog (Isa. 56:10): Barkless Baptists!
2. Dead Dog (1 Sam. 24:14; 2 Sam. 9:8; 16:9)
3. Disobedient, Deceived (Titus 3:3)
4. Doubtful Disputations (Rom. 14:1)
5. Divine Divinations (Ezek. 13:23)
6. Doctrine Defender (Jude 3)
7. Dogma Dispenser
8. Donated Dumbness
9. Dedicated Divine
10. Doctor of Divinity

Dispensations

Someone has said that if you believe God does different things at different times—you are a dispensationalist!

The Seven Dispensations Are:

1. Innocence
2. Conscience
3. Government
4. Promise
5. Law
6. Grace
7. Kingdom

There are five points to be considered in each dispensation (*oikonomia*: economy, stewardship, arrangement, plan) of God:

1. Man's condition
2. The Test
3. The Failure
4. The Judgment
5. The Way of Salvation—God's Way

Divine Analogies

Someone wrote, "I see in the red rose His blood." These words haunted me, and for several days I meditated upon the things we Christians may see in the handiwork and deeds of a loving Creator, our Father, and Jesus Christ our Savior. Here are my thoughts:

I see in the orbiting planets the upholding power of His word
I see in the galaxies the dust of His feet
I see in the firmament His handiwork—Ps. 19:1
I see in the brilliance of the sun His robe of majesty
I see in the earthquake the moving of His footstool

I see in the rainbow His mercy
I see in the tempestuous stormy sea the tranquility of His soul
I see in the lightning flash the blink of His eye
I see in the clouds His chariots and in the wind His wings
I see in the smoke of the volcanoes the touch of His finger—
    Ps. 104:32

I hear in the thunder the clapping of His hands
I see in the snowflake the vast treasures of His designs—Job 38:22

I see in the diving eagle the swiftness of His justice
I see in the whiteness of the snow sins that once were scarlet
I see in the blossoming desert His joy and gladness
I see in the setting up and casting down of kings His
    Sovereign rule
I see in every uplifted door the King of Glory—Ps. 24:9
I see in every earthen vessel a gospel treasure
I see in every fire His answer to prayer—1 Kings 18:24

I see in yea and amen His promises
I see in the raindrops His tears
I see in the human body, fearfully and wonderfully made, the
    marvel of His works—Ps. 139:14
I see in the purple violet His royalty
I see in the lily the beauty of His holiness

I see in the fresh-fallen drops of dew His favor—Prov. 19:12
I see in the grains of sand His innumerable thoughts—
    Ps. 139:18
I see in the crown of thorns His humility
I see in the empty tomb a living Savior

Oh! now I see the crimson wave, the fountain deep and wide;
    Jesus, my Lord, mighty to save, points to His wounded side.
The cleansing stream, I see, I see; I plunge, and oh, it cleanseth me!
    Oh! Praise the Lord, it cleanseth me; it cleanseth me, yes, cleanseth
    me!

—Phoebe P. Knapp

Divorce and Remarriage
Matthew 19:9–12

And I say to you, whoever divorces his wife, except for sexual immorality, and marries another, commits adultery; and whoever marries her who is divorced commits adultery.

The Sad Situation

In America today nearly two out of every four marriages end in divorce. This is a terrible percentage and indicates the sad spiritual condition of our nation. There seems to be little if any stigma attached to divorce. Even in our churches, ministers and deacons are divorced and nothing much is said against it. Folks married for 25 and 30 years call it quits and head for Splitsville.

Evil Influences

What are the reasons for this situation? That Satan is involved there is no doubt. And lust has its lodging place in man's heart. Undoubtedly we are influenced by Hollywood and by the soap operas that are heard and seen every afternoon and several evenings during the week. Other influences leading to the undermining of marriage are such things as: the use of the Pill and other contraceptives (an "eat your cake and keep it too" philosophy); the use of dope and alcohol; wild, suggestive music and dances; abortion clinics; homosexuality; shacking up and co-ed living and the lack of judgment preaching from our pulpits.

Confrontation

Now, as Christians, our concern is with what God's Word teaches about divorce and remarriage. We want then to base our study primarily upon Matthew 19:3–12, bringing in other scriptures as this passage is expounded. Immediately we see the setting is confrontation. The Pharisees were intent upon testing the Lord Jesus. Their desire was to get Him in trouble with the Law of Moses. Unfortunately for them, they did not realize Jesus Christ is the Perfecter of the Law.

And so they asked, "Is it lawful for a man to divorce his wife for just any reason?" The Lord answered, "Have you not read that He who made them at the beginning 'made them male and female,' and said, 'For this reason a man shall leave his father and mother and be joined to his wife, and the two shall become one flesh'?"

Homosexuality

Note first of all that God gave Eve to Adam. He did not give Steve to Adam. "Male and female He created them" (Gen. 1:27, 2:23–24). It is God's desire that this distinctiveness between male and female be maintained (even with respect to clothing, Deut. 22:5). Men have no business relating to men sexually, nor women with women. We are not biologically, physiologically or psychologically made that way. No amount of rationalization can change this fact. From a Biblical point of view, no one is born homosexual. It is a lifestyle that is acquired, learned. For the Bible believer the issue is clearly settled: Homosexuality is condemned (Gen. 19:5; Lev. 18:22, 20:13; Rom. 1:26–27; 1 Cor. 6:9 and 1 Tim. 1:10). The fact that half of the psychiatrists believe homosexuality is acquired and half of them do not, is not the basis for our position as Christians.

What holds weight for us is that the Bible utterly condemns homosexuality. And yet this word must be added: The Word of God offers hope to the sinner and includes among sinners the homosexual (1 Cor. 6:9–11). Advice is given in Matthew 19:4–5 for young married couples not to live with their parents or in-laws (Gen. 2:24; Eph. 5:31). And finally, these verses say that the two are to become one flesh, an impossibility for man with man, or woman with woman.

The Institution of Marriage

The Lord Jesus went on to point out in Matthew 19:6, "So then, they are no longer two, but one flesh. Therefore, what God has joined together, let not man separate." Here is a oneness that man is not to break up. But note it says **what**, not **who** God united. The relative pronoun used, a nominative and accusative singular **neuter**, suggests that it is the institution of marriage that is the issue. And the tense (*aorist*) of the verb rendered "joined together" refers to the historical act of giving Eve to Adam.

In other words, marriage is of God. He instituted it when He gave Eve to Adam. Some ministers state that if God did not put you together, then it is all right to get a divorce. Such teaching cannot be supported by Matthew 19:6 or proven from the New Testament. The point is: Since marriage is of God—started, instituted by Him—nobody has a right to interfere with your marriage.

According to Hebrews 13:4, all marriage is honorable; marriage is honorable in all. Why? Because it was started, instituted, initiated, established, set up by God; it is divine. So whether that marriage is polygamous, interracial, between tall and short, or fat and skinny, Protestant and Roman Catholic, light skin and dark skin, rich and poor, old and young, two unbelievers or even between a Christian and an unbeliever—*once married*, that marriage is sacred. Yes, even the marriage of a divorced person!

No Divorce

Now Matthew 19:7 clearly indicates the Pharisees understood that Christ taught no divorce. This is why they said to Him, "Why then did Moses command to give a certificate of divorce, and to put her away?" (Deut. 24:1–4). He said to them, "Moses, because of the hardness of your hearts, permitted you to divorce your wives, but from the beginning it was not so" (Matt. 19:8).

Skip now to Matthew 19:10 and see once again that the disciples understood the Lord said no divorce. "His disciples said to Him, 'If such is the case of the man with his wife, it is better not to marry.'" In other words, "Lord, if a man cannot get rid of a woman when he wants to, it is best for him not to get married at all." Such is their masculine arrogance, an attitude concerning women that is typical of their tradition.

The Lord answered: "All cannot accept this saying, but only those to whom it has been given. For there are eunuchs who were born thus from their mother's womb, and there are eunuchs who were made eunuchs by men, and there are eunuchs who have made themselves eunuchs for the kingdom of heaven's sake. He who is able to accept it, let him accept it" (Matt. 19:11–12).

Now up to this point the Lord Jesus has said "no divorce." Marriage is to be a permanent relationship. That God hates divorce is strongly stated in Malachi 2:15–16, where "putting away" (KJV) means divorce. Because the Bible is the Word of God and does not contradict itself, we can rest assured that we shall not find any scriptures elsewhere to make divorce something that is approved by God.

Significance of Betrothal

Look now at the key verse, Matthew 19:9: "And I say to you, whoever divorces his wife, except for sexual immorality, and marries another, commits adultery; and whoever marries her who is divorced commits adultery." First keep in mind that Matthew's Gospel had the Jews in view; Mark's Gospel (10:1–12) had the Romans in mind; and Luke's Gospel (16:18) had the Greeks in mind. Among the Jews was the custom called betrothal. "Troth" means faith, pledged faith: "I pledge thee my troth!" Betrothal means to engage or promise in marriage; it is a mutual contract for a future marriage. Note, a betrothed woman is called a wife in Deuteronomy 22:23–24.

When a young Jewish man desired to marry a Jewish girl, the parents got together, talked things over and decided when the marriage should take place. Money was exchanged at a ceremony, a paper or document was signed, and publicly the man and the woman were declared betrothed. Then the daughter would go back home with her parents, and the son would go back home with his parents. But as far as the Jewish law was concerned, they were married. Then about a year would be spent in preparation for the public wedding which would take place.

And during that time there would be no sexual contact at all between the two. Yet, according to their law, even though no sexual contact consummated the marriage to that point, they were married to each other.

Fornication and Adultery

Note the Lord did not say here, "Whosoever shall put away his wife, except it be for *adultery*." For under the Law adultery was punishable by death by stoning (Exod. 20:14; Lev. 20:10). Adultery is the violation of another person's marriage and is not quite the same as "fornication," the word found in the KJV. Both adultery and fornication are the same physically, both are acts of sexual immorality. But adultery is committed by a person whose marriage has been consummated and cannot be committed by anyone who is simply betrothed. The word *fornication* used here is of that sexual relationship by people who are betrothed or engaged. It is premarital impurity, even though by Jewish custom those betrothed were considered married. Fornication had varying penalties.

Thus Matthew 19:9 deals with unfaithfulness on the part of the one betrothed or engaged. If the woman has sex with someone during that time of betrothal, then and only then has the man the right to put her away, according to this Jewish custom. See this very clearly in the life of Mary and Joseph. According to Matthew 1:18, Mary was espoused, betrothed, pledged to be married to Joseph. But before they came together, while still in that betrothal period, Mary was found to be pregnant. Because Joseph her husband was a righteous man, and did not want to expose her to public disgrace, he had in mind to divorce her quietly.

It is safe to say that in Matthew 19:9 the Lord shows what happens when a Jewish man breaks off his betrothal. To the Jew the betrothal was binding, much more serious than our engagements today. He could not back out of it and please God. Unless it is discovered the bride-to-be was guilty of fornication (sex with someone else prior to or during this engagement period), he could not get out of the marriage.

Remarriage

The question comes now: What about divorce and remarriage? It is unfortunate that certain passages have been rendered in such a way that some people have interpreted divorce to be an unforgivable sin and consider remarriage as constituting adultery. In Mark 10:11–12 (NASB) we read: "And He said to them, 'Whoever divorces His wife and marries another woman commits adultery against her; and if she herself divorces her husband and marries another man, she is committing adultery.'"

Disruption of the marriage relationship is sin. Divorce is sin. The man who divorces and remarries aggravates his situation; for remember, Christ dealt here primarily with the violation of the Seventh Commandment. Men deliberately divorced their wives so that they could have other women. Discussion about the bill of divorcement in Deuteronomy 24:1–4 is not the heart of the matter.

In Mark 10:11–12, the primary aim is to bring out the sin which the divorcer commits against *himself* or *herself.* Remember this! In the Matthew scripture (Matt. 5:31–32, 19:9), emphasis is upon the sin the divorcer perpetrates against *others*. However, Mark stresses the evil committed by the divorcer against himself or herself.

Because the verb *moichatai* may be passive, it may be rendered, "he is made adulterous" rather than the active, "he commits adultery." Thus the man who divorces his wife and marries another woman is made adulterous in regard to his first wife. And if the wife divorces her husband and marries another man, she is made adulterous. Mark writes for the Gentile, and this is why mention is made of the wife initiating the divorce against her husband. The usual case for the Jews was for the husband to file for the divorce. But no matter who initiated the disruption, the act was sin. And it is this sin—the destruction of marriage—that begins in the lust of the heart and makes one adulterous.

Consider now Matthew 5:32 (NASB): "But I say to you that everyone who divorces his wife, except for the reason of unchastity, makes her commit adultery; and whoever marries a divorced woman commits adultery." Here injury done to others is the main thrust. Whereas in Mark 10:11–12 stress is upon the harm the divorcer does to himself or herself, in Matthew 5:32 the major emphasis is the sin the divorcer commits (1) against his wife and (2) against the man who later may marry that woman. Christ wants it seen that a man who breaks up a marriage is guilty of violating the will and Word of God. By obtaining the divorce he forces his wife into a position which appears contrary to the Seventh Commandment: he puts her in a position of being stigmatized as adulterous. The phrases "makes her commit adultery" and "commits adultery" are better changed from the active to the passive. Indeed, the word *moicheuthenai* is an aorist infinitive *passive*.

It should be obvious to the reader that it is not possible for a man to divorce his wife and *cause* her or *make* her an adulteress. He is the one who has committed the evil. The moment he drives her out—whether or not she remarries—she is "marked" as adulterous. Christ does not forbid the divorced person to remarry. But there is a stigma put upon her by the act of her evil husband.

Paul would say in First Corinthians 7:15 that the woman thus driven out is under no bondage. She is free from the marriage which her lustful husband broke up. However, if she does remarry, her new husband shares her stigma—married to a woman whose former marriage was destroyed by her former husband.

To cause one to commit adultery is one thing. To stigmatize or characterize one as adulterous is another matter. I repeat: Divorce does not cause her to commit adultery. Such an idea is untenable. The problem in part is that in English we do not have passive rendering that corresponds to the active rendering. Put yourself in Jewish society at that time. There comes down the street a woman recently divorced. What goes through your mind? That she committed adultery, and that's why her husband divorced her. Admittedly, this concept may be due to the demand for unconditional fidelity made only on the part of the woman. After all, in marriage she was the possession of her husband. Of course Christ changed this, and the man's right to sexual freedom was denied. In Christ, husband and wife are heirs together of God's good grace. And marriage is a lifelong partnership as was originally, ideally intended.

You can see now that the correct rendering of the remainder of Matthew 5:32 is not "whosoever shall marry her that is divorced commits adultery," but that "whoever marries the woman thus divorced is likewise stigmatized as adulterous." In the Jewish community the divorced woman was forced into a position that made it appear she had violated the Seventh Commandment (Exod. 20:14).

In summary: Neither the divorced woman nor the man who marries her commits anything. Something is committed against them. What is it? Stigma. A mark of reproach and disgrace. The shadow of a disrupted, destroyed, broken marriage follows them.

Does Divorce Unsave?

Have you ever heard it said that a person divorced and re-married was living in adultery? How ridiculous! If such an interpretation is correct, then according to First Corinthians 6:9–10, all divorced and remarried folks are lost and on their way to hell! No, my friends, divorce does not unsave anyone. "For such were some of you; but ye are washed, but ye are sanctified, but ye are justified in the name of the Lord Jesus, and by the Spirit of our God" (1 Cor. 6:11, KJV). There are no scriptures which put divorced/remarried people in hell simply because they are divorced and remarried.

All have sinned (past tense) and are falling (present tense) short of God's glory. Some of us got into trouble after we were saved. God in Christ has forgiven us. Now it is a fact that though we are forgiven, our forgiven sins have lingering effects. The scars are still there. One lung may be missing because of cigarette smoking. I may walk with a limp because of an automobile accident which occurred when I was drunk while driving.

Some folks get belligerent after drinking and like to fight. A man got his eye knocked out that way. He is saved but he is a one-eyed Christian. The baby born out of wedlock is a fine-looking high school senior now. I wonder if you see my point? I am forgiven, but the results of my past sins may still linger. Reminders may still be present. And though forgiven, some sins may cause me to forfeit certain privileges in life. I should think it is the guy who wants to eat his cake and keep it too who is most offended by this truth.

What About Remarriage?

I have discovered some fundamentalist pastors and church members are very harsh in their beliefs about this matter. It is dangerous to go beyond what the Bible does teach and insist that our beliefs, our interpretations and opinions are the only correct ones. And no matter how dogmatic I am, no matter how strongly I hold to my convictions, there is no excuse for me not to pray, study and seek Holy Spirit enlightenment.

Take, for example, the belief that the woman belongs to the man with whom she first had sex. Such an idea ignores incest or rape. It puts a burden upon the woman and none upon the man. Are women whose husbands divorced them doomed to loneliness, never again to marry? Shall the Christian man who is divorced remain unmarried the rest of his life? I do not hold to such ideas. Nor did the Old Testament. In Deuteronomy 24:2 (KJV) we read: "And when she is departed out of his house, she may go and be another man's wife." This verse devastates the belief held by some that remarriage of the divorced is forbidden.

Under the Law in Israel it was not forbidden. Why should it be under grace in the church? Thus it is evil to suggest that a divorced person who remarries then has two living spouses. Such an opinion does not value the meaning of words. Note the words "her former husband" (Deut. 24:4). Divorce means divorce!— separation, loosing, breakup, split, sundered, destruction, dissolution, release, dismissal, disruption. We cannot possibly deduce correctly that disrupted marriage is still in God's sight a binding marriage. It is not. Whereas the disruption is evil, and is condemned as such, God in no place forbids the innocent party to marry again. And as for the guilty party, there is always room for repentance.

Adultery With Your Wife?

You cannot truthfully be accused of living in adultery with the one to whom you are married. Not by our definition of adultery. Now Romans 7:2–3 (NASB) must not be misinterpreted:

> For the married woman is bound by law to her husband while he is living; but if her husband dies, she is released from the law concerning the husband. So then, if while her husband is living, she is joined to another man, she shall be called an adulteress; but if her husband dies, she is free from the law, so that she is not an adulteress, though she is joined to another man.

The weight falls on the words "her husband." If she is divorced is he still her husband? If you say yes, then you will have problems with this issue. If you believe that a disrupted marriage is still a marriage in God's sight, then you will forever have problems with this matter of divorce and remarriage. But if you believe that the divorced party is no longer the husband, no longer the wife, then we can move on. And we will not interpret divorce and remarriage to be adultery.

Pastoral Procedure

What is my procedure as a pastor? First, I seek the possibility of reconciliation. For the ideal is that the two come back together. But sometimes this is impossible: (1) the whereabouts of one party may be unknown, or (2) the other party has remarried. Second, I warn the divorced Christian that he or she is obligated to marry only a believer. And third, I remind the man, if he is the divorced person, that he may not be allowed to hold certain positions in some churches or denominations.

For example: First Timothy 3:2,12 is interpreted to mean that a pastor or a deacon is to be the husband of one wife. Even this is complicated because some scholars interpret the phrase "a one-wife kind of a man" to suggest an attitude, a lifestyle, a belief held even by a divorced man (whose first wife may have initiated the divorce). Other scholars see these verses only as prohibitions against polygamy.

Not Under Bondage?

To say a divorced Christian cannot remarry or should not remarry is not to my mind my prerogative. And I do not believe it is yours! Now to those contemplating divorce who come to me, I always advise that they strive to live pleasing to Jesus Christ even in a bad situation: pray, talk things over, counsel, try to make a go of it. I recognize that we live in an imperfect world. Some of us back ourselves into situations where the believer has to choose between two evils, hopefully the lesser. Divorce could be that lesser evil. I may advise leaving, but I do not under any circumstances tell folks to seek a divorce. Divorce is wrong. But the decision of what to do is not mine to make. If leaving is suggested, it is only according to First Corinthians 7:10–15, where the idea is that conversion to Jesus Christ is no basis for divorcing an unbelieving spouse. I always tell the believer, you do what is right, and the Lord will fight your battles.

He will undertake for you. If the other party wants to do wrong, and initiates the divorce, let him, or her. You cannot make anybody love you or stay with you. My policy has been if the other party divorces and remarries, you are free. Free to do what? Paul does not say in First Corinthians 7:15. Let the Holy Spirit guide you.

The burden of guilt and sin is upon the other party, not you. I recognize too that it is not automatically always wise for a divorced person to remarry. But it may well be the Lord's will for you. How many of you are working right now on something that is God's first will for your lives? His tenth will? His ninety-ninth will?

Summary

We have argued for the inviolability of marriage. The Lord Jesus is concerned with our hearts. Note this brethren, in Matthew 5:27–28 Christ is concerned with the morality issue involved in divorce. God hates divorce. And so we have taught. No divorce! But if and when there is divorce, what then? Pick up the pieces and go on from there.

If reconciliation is impossible, seek the Lord's will for your life. Do not feel guilty or think it impossible that He might lead you to a good Christian spouse. It is possible. It has happened.

By God's grace some second marriages are wonderful, really blessed and honorable in God's sight (Heb. 13:4).

Like all sins divorce leaves scars, so be willing to face problems that come up because of past divorce or present remarriage. Confess your mistake, thank the Lord for His forgiveness of all sins (past, present and future), and go on in the name of Jesus Christ who shed His blood for you!

Easter Dates

Year	Easter Sunday
2007	April 8
2008	March 23
2009	April 12
2010	April 4
2011	April 24
2012	April 8
2013	March 31
2014	April 20
2015	April 5
2016	March 27
2017	April 16
2018	April 1
2019	April 21
2020	April 12
2021	April 4
2022	April 17
2023	April 9
2024	March 31

Funerals

FUNERAL POLICY

Membership should be reminded periodically at church meetings and other services of the policy of the church regarding funerals. For example, the family of the deceased should contact the pastor *before* setting dates for the funeral service. Funerals require a coordinated effort from the pastor, mortician, sexton, musicians, choirs and choruses, and the family. Failure to get the approval of the minister with respect to the date and time of the services may lead to a mix-up and cause disappointment and hard feelings.

If it is the policy of the church *not* to have a second viewing of the remains, there should indeed be no exceptions. Morticians should be made aware of the church's rule and inform the family. It is my belief that there should be no second viewing at the church. Too often I have seen such an emotional outburst at the time of the second viewing that it seemed the sermon preached was in vain. Certainly nothing is gained spiritually by subjecting the family and friends to repeat such a ritual.

Fraternal organizations should schedule their ceremonies *before* the Christian church service and be finished in time for those who come later to view the body before the church service commences. Some churches prepare food for the family and friends of the deceased and hold a repast after returning from the cemetery. The cost is usually borne by the church. But other churches leave it up to the club, auxiliary or board to which the deceased belonged, to bear the expenses voluntarily and to purchase food, prepare it and serve. Either way, a church policy should be set.

Finally, some pastors have made it their rule that they alone will preach the eulogy of the deceased member, thus excluding former or emeritus pastors from doing the eulogy. The wisdom of such a policy is questionable. If the family requests a minister other then the pastor, I acquiesce, although my concern would be that he preach the gospel of Jesus Christ. In case another minister preaches the eulogy, the pastor should be the presiding officer. In this way he may control the service and guard the pulpit with final remarks and benediction.

SHOULD NON-MEMBERS BE FUNERALIZED AT THE CHURCH?

Two men stood in a funeral parlor viewing the body of a deceased friend named Sam. One man began to laugh and when questioned, replied: "You know, Sam didn't believe in a heaven or in a hell. And I was just thinking—here he is all dressed up and no place to go!" As you know, in the early church Christians often met in secret in homes (1 Cor. 16:19). Persecution was in part responsible for this. In time, as the faith became more acceptable, the church moved out into special buildings.

Naturally their doors were open to all, but only professed Christians operated the church. And this is as it should be—God's church run by God's people. Only true Christians are in the invisible body of Christ, the church; so only true believers ought to constitute the membership of the visible body. It is the place where saints come together to fellowship, pray, study the Bible, take Communion, praise and worship Jesus Christ.

A pastor and people therefore have every right to exclude non-members from participation in the affairs of the church. As for the issue at hand, pastors have the right to deny holding obsequies of non-members on church property. Certainly as Baptists we respect the autonomy of each local assembly. People who are not members of that particular church have no right to tell that local assembly how to run its business.

Understand that I do not condemn pastors or churches which refuse to funeralize non-members in their church edifices. The church is for its church members. Not for unbelievers. Not for non-members. And not for folks all dressed up with no place to go! I personally permit the funerals of non-members to be held in the church if it is the request of those in the family who are members. No one compels me or demands it. And I reserve the right to refuse (a bartender, for example).

Sometimes these non-members are backslidden Christians who have died out of fellowship with the church. This is as much a possibility as it is that a member in good standing in the church has never been born again. Having the funeral of a known unbeliever in the church does not necessarily reflect inconsistency.

Living unbelievers attend every Sunday, some even contribute to the offering (though I never encourage known unbelievers to give anything). So I see no harm in having a few dead ones brought in, especially if I do not attempt to put the deceased in heaven just to please the family and friends.

We should not quote, "Let the dead bury the dead" (Matt. 8:22). Let the spiritually dead bury the physically dead is the meaning. To cite this scripture but then conduct the funeral at the mortician's place means you are still included among the "spiritually dead" ones. Consistency would require (according to such mistaken use of this verse) that we have nothing to do with the funerals of unbelievers.

The verse must be kept in its context. Christ's claim and call have precedence over the claims of tradition or society, possibly involving even the abandonment of human relations. For many pastors it is seen as an opportunity to preach the gospel of the shed blood of Jesus Christ to people who may never hear it again. In conclusion: I put the issue in the category of the pragmatic. It is not to me a matter of right or wrong. Each pastor should do what he feels led to do. Under no circumstances should he be put under an obligation to funeralize or not to funeralize in the church people who are not members of the church.

CREMATION

The practice of cremation is growing in the United States, and there are a number of reasons for this trend. Cemetery space is becoming more and more limited. Families desire to keep down funeral costs. It is true that cremation is currently less expensive than the usual procedure of interring the embalmed body. One suspects, however, that as the frequency of using cremation increases, the cost, in accord with American economic policy, will also increase!

Cremation is but a hastening or speeding up of the process of disintegration and corruption which normally takes place after death. We return to the ground, "for dust you are, and to dust you shall return" (Gen. 3:19). Perhaps the incident that is foremost in our minds is the burning of the body of king Saul (1 Sam. 31:12). After Saul killed himself, his enemies found his body and the corpses of his three sons.

They cut off his head, stripped off his armor and fastened his body to the wall of Beth Shan. When the valiant men of Jabesh-Gilead heard what the Philistines had done to Saul, they took down the bodies, burned them and buried the bones under the tamarisk tree at Jabesh (1 Chron. 10:11–12).

Such burning was not the usual custom of the Israelites, but possibly the Jews feared the Philistines would remove the bodies and further mutilate and desecrate them. Decapitated bodies made impossible any way a regular burial. Other instances of burning are examples of *capital punishment*. Achan and his family were stoned to death and burned with fire (Josh. 7:15, 25). A man who marries a woman and her mother—they shall all be burned with fire (Lev. 20:14). And the priest's daughter who plays the harlot, profaning herself and her father, shall be burned with fire (Lev. 21:9).

These incidents of burning bodies do not negate the fact that it was Israel's custom to bury corpses in the ground, not burn them. There appears then to be no instance in the Bible of approved cremation of a believer's body. And I must admit I am opposed to cremation. However, I do not refuse to participate in funeral services involving cremation. To me cremation smacks of paganism. It seems to be a failure to recognize or appreciate the fact that the Christian's body was the temple of the Holy Spirit.

Cremation seems—I know this is highly subjective—fatalistic, almost on an animal level, as if to say, this is it! You're done! Reference to dead believers as being "asleep" makes cremation appear to me to be an inappropriate option for disposing of the remains, especially for all who still believe in the imminent return of the Lord Jesus Christ.

SUICIDE

Suicide or self-murder is an immoral act. It is an example of an extreme act of rebellion against God, a striking out at the Creator. The idea that suicide is the unpardonable, unforgivable sin persists, but there is no scriptural basis for believing it is impossible for a genuine Christian to commit suicide, or for suggesting the Christian who does commit suicide loses his or her salvation. Neither is it proper to suggest the doctrine of eternal security condones suicide.

Seven instances of suicide are recorded in the Bible: (1) Abimelech, Judges 9:54; actually, he requested his armor-bearer to thrust him through with the sword, and his servant obeyed;

(2) Samson, Judges 16:30; (3) and (4) Saul and his armor-bearer, 1 Samuel 31:4–5; (5) Ahithophel, 2 Samuel 17:23; (6) Zimri, 1 Kings 16:18; (7) Judas, Matthew 27:5. The jailer in Acts 16:27 was prevented by Paul and Silas from killing himself. And certain of the earth-dwellers of the Tribulation age will be unable to kill themselves, Revelation 9:6.

I have no compelling reasons for refusing to conduct the funeral of a suicide victim; and I would not deny the funeral services being held in the church. There are those whose minds become deranged and they take their own lives. Christians are not immune to depression, despondency or mental illness. For statistics on the growing rate of suicide among Black Americans, especially young Blacks, see the latest available *Vital Statistics of the U.S.*, the volume on Mortality.

FUNERAL SCRIPTURES:

TO BE READ WHILE LEADING THE FAMILY INTO THE CHURCH

Deut. 33:27: The eternal God is your refuge, and underneath are the everlasting arms.

Job 1:21: Naked I came from my mother's womb, and naked shall I return there. The Lord gave, and the Lord has taken away; blessed be the name of the Lord.

Job 14:1–2: Man who is born of woman is of few days, and full of trouble. He comes forth like a flower and fades away; he flees like a shadow and does not continue.

Job 19:25–27: For I know that my Redeemer lives, and He shall stand at last on the earth; and after my skin is destroyed, this I know, that in my flesh I shall see God, whom I shall see for myself, and my eyes shall behold, and not another.

Ps. 23: The Lord is my shepherd; I shall not want. He makes me to lie down in green pastures; He leads me beside the still waters. He restores my soul; He leads me in the paths of righteousness for His name's sake. Yea, though I walk through the valley of the shadow of death, I will fear no evil; for You are with me; Your rod and Your staff they comfort me. You prepare a table before me in the presence of my enemies; You anoint my head with oil; my cup runs over. Surely goodness and mercy shall follow me all the days of my life; and I will dwell in the house of the Lord forever.

Ps. 27:1: The Lord is my light and my salvation; whom shall I fear? The Lord is the strength of my life; of whom shall I be afraid?

Ps. 39:4–6: Lord, make me to know my end, and what is the measure of my days, that I may know how frail I am. Indeed, You have made my days as handbreadths, and my age is as nothing before You; certainly every man at his best state is but vapor. Surely every man walks about like a shadow; surely they busy themselves in vain; he heaps up riches, and does not know who will gather them.

Ps. 46:1–3,10: God is our refuge and strength, a very present help in trouble. Therefore we will not fear, even though the earth be removed, and though the mountains be carried into the midst of the sea; though its waters roar and be troubled, though the mountains shake with its swelling. . . . Be still, and know that I am God.

Ps. 56:3–4: Whenever I am afraid, I will trust in You. In God (I will praise His word), in God I have put my trust; I will not fear. What can flesh do to me?

Ps. 90:1–12: Lord, You have been our dwelling place in all generations. Before the mountains were brought forth, or ever You had formed the earth and the world, even from everlasting to everlasting, You are God. You turn man to destruction, and say, "Return, O children of men." For a thousand years in Your sight are like yesterday when it is past, and like a watch in the night. You carry them away like a flood; they are like a sleep. In the morning they are like grass which grows up; in the morning it flourishes and grows up; in the evening it is cut down and withers. For we have been consumed by Your anger, and by Your wrath we are terrified. You have set our iniquities before You, our secret sins in the light of Your countenance. For all our days have passed away in Your wrath; we finish our years like a sigh. The days of our lives are seventy years; and if by reason of strength they are eighty years, yet their boast is only labor and sorrow; for it is soon cut off, and we fly away. Who knows the power of Your anger? For as the fear of You, so is Your wrath. So teach us to number our days, that we may gain a heart of wisdom.

Ps. 121: I will lift up my eyes to the hills—from whence comes my help? My help comes from the Lord, who made heaven and earth. He will not allow your foot to be moved; He who keeps you will not slumber. Behold, He who keeps

Israel shall neither slumber nor sleep. The Lord is your keeper; the Lord is your shade at your right hand. The sun shall not strike you by day, nor the moon by night. The Lord shall preserve you from all evil; He shall preserve your soul. The Lord shall preserve your going out and your coming in from this time forth, and even forever more.

John 11:25–26: Jesus said to her, "I am the resurrection and the life. He who believes in Me, though he may die, he shall live. And whoever lives and believes in Me shall never die."

John 14:1–6: Let not your heart be troubled; you believe in God, believe also in Me. In My Father's house are many mansions; if it were not so, I would have told you. I go to prepare a place for you. And if I go and prepare a place for you, I will come again and receive you to Myself; that where I am, there you may be also. And where I go you know, and the way you know. Thomas said to Him, "Lord, we do not know where You are going, and how can we know the way?" Jesus said to him, "I am the way, the truth, and the life. No one comes to the Father except through Me."

Rom. 8:28, 31–39: And we know that all things work together for good to those who love God, to those who are the called according to His purpose. . . . What then shall we say to these things? If God is for us, who can be against us? He who did not spare His own Son, but delivered Him up for us all, how shall He not with Him also freely give us all things? Who shall bring a charge against God's elect? It is God who justifies. Who is he who condemns? It is Christ who died, and furthermore is also risen, who is even at the right hand of God, who also makes intercession for us. Who shall separate us from the love of Christ? Shall tribulation, or distress, or persecution, or famine, or nakedness, or peril, or sword? As it is written: "For Your sake we are killed all day long; we are accounted as sheep for the slaughter." Yet in all these things we are more than conquerors through Him who loved us. For I am persuaded that neither death nor life, nor angels nor principalities nor powers, nor things present nor things to come, nor height nor depth, nor any other created thing, shall be able to separate us from the love of God which is in Christ Jesus our Lord.

1 Cor. 15:50–58: Now this I say, brethren, that flesh and blood cannot inherit the kingdom of God; nor does corruption inherit incorruption. Behold, I tell you a mystery: We shall not all sleep, but we shall all be changed—in a moment, in the twinkling of an eye, at the last trumpet. For the trumpet will sound, and the dead will be raised incorruptible, and we shall be changed. For this corruptible must put on incorruption, and this mortal must put on immortality. So when this corruptible has put on incorruption, and this mortal has put on immortality, then shall be brought to pass the saying that is written: "Death is swallowed up in victory. O Death, where is your sting? O Hades, where is your victory?" The sting of death is sin, and the strength of sin is the law. But thanks be to God, who gives us the victory through our Lord Jesus Christ. Therefore, my beloved brethren, be steadfast, immovable, always abounding in the work of the Lord, knowing that your labor is not in vain in the Lord.

2 Cor. 4:17–18; 5:1: For our light affliction, which is but for a moment, is working for us a far more exceeding and eternal weight of glory, while we do not look at the things which are seen, but at the things which are not seen. For the things which are seen are temporary, but the things which are not seen are eternal. For we know that if our earthly house, this tent, is destroyed, we have a building from God, a house not made with hands, eternal in the heavens.

1 Thess. 4:13–18: But I do not want you to be ignorant, brethren, concerning those who have fallen asleep, lest you sorrow as others who have no hope. For if we believe that Jesus died and rose again, even so God will bring with Him those who sleep in Jesus. For this we say to you by the word of the Lord, that we who are alive and remain until the coming of the Lord will by no means precede those who are asleep. For the Lord Himself will descend from heaven with a shout, with the voice of an archangel, and with the trumpet of God. And the dead in Christ will rise first. Then we who are alive and remain shall be caught up together with them in the clouds to meet the Lord in the air. And thus we shall always be with the Lord. Therefore comfort one another with these words.

2 Tim. 4:6–8: For I am already being poured out as a drink offering, and the time of my departure is at hand. I have fought the good fight, I have finished the race, I have kept the faith. Finally, there is laid up for me the crown of righteousness, which the Lord, the righteous judge, will give to me on that Day, and not to me only but also to all who have loved His appearing.

Rev. 7:15–17: Therefore they are before the throne of God, and serve Him day and night in His temple. And He who sits on the throne will dwell among them. They shall neither hunger anymore nor thirst anymore; the sun shall not strike them, nor any heat; for the Lamb who is in the midst of the throne will shepherd them and lead them to living fountains of waters. And God will wipe away every tear from their eyes.

Rev. 21:1–5: I saw a new heaven and a new earth, for the first heaven and the first earth had passed away. Also there was no more sea. Then I, John, saw the holy city, New Jerusalem, coming down out of heaven from God, prepared as a bride adorned for her husband. And I heard a loud voice from heaven saying, "Behold, the tabernacle of God is with men, and He will dwell with them, and they shall be His people. And God Himself will be with them and be their God. And God will wipe away every tear from their eyes; there shall be no more death, nor sorrow, nor crying; and there shall be no more pain, for the former things have passed away." Then He who sat on the throne said, "Behold, I make all things new." And He said to me, "Write, for these words are true and faithful."

FUNERAL SERVICE: A SIMPLE, BASIC OUTLINE

Meeting the family at the entrance of the church, the pastor requests those seated in the audience to rise. In order for the reading of the Scriptures to be heard, the musician stops playing. The pastor then leads the family in as he reads appropriate scriptures. Once the family is seated, the audience is requested also to be seated. At the proper time, the final viewing is made; the casket is closed. There should be no second viewing after the eulogy.* The pastor then proceeds:

Opening Hymn
Scripture: Old Testament and New Testament
Prayer
Hymn
Condolence and Resolutions
Remarks
Hymn
Obituary
Eulogy
Committal** (*See bottom of next page*)
Benediction
Closing Hymn: As the minister leads the family out.

---

* Deacons, visiting and associate ministers may be assigned the task of presiding, reading the Scriptures, praying, and under proper instructions, in bringing remarks. The church clerk usually reads the condolences and resolutions.

Pastors may read the obituary, assign someone else to do it or have it read silently.

FUNERAL TEXTS

Gen. 5:24: He walked with God

Gen. 15:15: A Good Old Age (*Gen. 25:8; 1 Chron. 29:28*)

Exod. 12:30: Death in Every House (*Jer. 9:21*)

Num. 21:9: Look and Live! (*Prov. 4:4:* Obey and Live; *Luke 10:28:* Love and Live; *John 6:50:* Eat and Live). These four points could be used in a sermon entitled, How to Live Though Born to Die.

Deut. 33:27: God our Refuge (Everlasting Arms)

Josh. 1:5: A Friend Who Never Fails

Josh. 23:14: A Soldier's Death

1 Sam. 1:28: On Loan

1 Sam. 3:8: A Child Called by God

1 Sam. 13:14: A Man After God's Own Heart (*Ps. 89:20; Acts 13:22*)

1 Sam. 20:3: A Step Between Life and Death

2 Sam. 1:26: Death of a Close Friend (*John 11:23*)

2 Sam. 12:23: Hope of Reunion

2 Sam. 18:33: Mourning for a Son (*Luke 7:12*)

2 Sam. 19:36: Over Jordan (*Josh. 1:11, 4:23*)

1 Kings 2:2–3: The Way of All the Earth

1 Kings 17:17: The Widow's Child (*Luke 7:12*)

** The pastor should make every effort to accompany the family to the cemetery and make the committal there before the interment. In extremely inclement weather, the pastor may make the committal in the church, then go with the family to the cemetery where no further ceremony would be performed.

Ps. 37:37: The End of a Man (*see also Job 6:11, 42:12*)

Ps. 39:4: My End, My Days, My Frailty (The End of My Way)

Ps. 40:2: God Who Lifts Up (Joseph, *Gen. 37:28; Jonah 2:6; Jeremiah 38:13*; the Lord Jesus, *John 3:13; 12:32*)

Ps. 40:3: A Tuned Heart, Loosed Tongue, Discerning Ear (Appropriate for the death of a musician or singer)

Ps. 46:1: Right Now Help in Right Now Trouble

Ps. 48:14: Guide unto Death

Ps. 49:17: What Follows?

Ps. 55:6: I'll Fly Away (*Isa. 60:8; Job 20:8*)

Ps. 68:5: Holy Habitation: His Heavenly Home (Father of the Fatherless)

Ps. 84:11: Profile of an Upright Man

Ps. 89:48: Seeing Death

Ps. 90:6: Life's Swift Transition (Hymn: God's Unchanging Hand)

Ps. 90:10: Soon Gone! (When I Fly Away): Sown, Grown, Mown, Blown, Gone!

Ps. 90:12: Numbered Days (I sometimes multiply the number of years the deceased lived by 365, plus leap years. For example, 60 years would be approximately 21,915 days)

Ps. 90:14: Readiness for Death Rejoices Life (*Eccl. 11:9*)

Ps. 91:16: Satisfied, Shown, Saved

Ps. 92:14: Portrait of a Remarkable Christian

Ps. 102:1–2: Hear, Don't Hide

Ps. 102:24: In the Midst of Life (*Isa. 38:10*)

Ps. 103:14–16: Frames of Dust

Ps. 116:8: A Three-fold Deliverance: My Soul from Death, My Eyes from Tears, My Foot from Falling

Ps. 116:15: Precious Death

Ps. 120:1: My Circumstances, My Cry, My Confidence

Ps. 133:3: Life Forevermore

Ps. 146:8: Now I See! (*John 9:25*)

Prov. 4:18: The Coming of a Perfect Day

Prov. 10:7: Blessed Memories

Prov. 11:18: Sow Right, Sure Reward

Prov. 14:32: Hope in Death

Prov. 15:24: The Path of Life (*Ps. 16:11; Matt 7:14*)

Prov. 16:31: Crown of Glory (Old Age: *Prov. 20:29*)

Prov. 18:24: The Death of a Dear Friend

Prov. 31:10–12: A Good Wife

Prov. 31:20: A Woman Who Helped

Prov. 31:31: A Life of Good Works

Eccl. 3:1–2: A Time for Everything

Eccl. 3:20: Dust to Dust (*Gen. 3:19*)

Eccl. 7:4: The House of Mourning (see Living Bible or Today's English Version: Good News Bible)

Eccl. 11:4–6: No Seedtime, No Harvest

Eccl. 11:9: Judgment Awaits Young People, Too!

Eccl. 12:1: The Days of Your Youth

Song of Sol. 6:2: Gathered Lilies

Isa. 11:6: Little Leaders (Be careful of the context)

Isa. 25:8: No More Death (*1 Cor. 15:26*)

Matt. 26:10: A Good Work for the Lord
Mark 4:35: Crossing Over
Mark 5:35: Death of a Daughter
Mark 10:13–16: Death of a Baby or Young Child
Mark 16:3–4: Stone-Rolling Time
Mark 16:10: Why Cry?
Luke 2:29–30: Departing in Peace: Release, Revelation, Reward
Luke 6:21: Weep Now, Laugh Later
Luke 7:14: Raising a Young Man
Luke 8:52: Weeping or Sleeping?
Luke 12:20: Who Gets What's Left? (You Can't Take It with You)
Luke 12:40: Be Ready!
Luke 16:23: In Hell He Lifted Up His Eyes
Luke 20:36: No More Death!
John 5:25–29: Which Will It Be?
John 6:37: Guaranteed
John 8:32: Free at Last!
John 8:51–52: Seeing Death (Tasting Death)
John 9:4: Night Comes
John 11:25: You Shall Never Die
John 11:33–35: Christ Weeps with You
John 12:24: Fruit in Death
John 13:7: Understand It Better By and By
John 14:1, 27: Untroubled Heart
John 14:2: Plenty Good Room
John 14:2: A Place Prepared
John 14:3: Come with Me!

John 14:17–18: Never Deserted, Never Orphaned!

John 16:22: Sorrow Turned to Joy

John 17:4: When Life's Work Is Ended

Acts 9:36: A Woman of Good Works

Acts 17:31: The Assured Appointment

Acts 21:14: Can You say, "Thy Will Be Done"? (*Matt. 6:10*)

Rom. 6:8: Dead But Alive (*2 Tim. 2:11*)

Rom. 8:18: Yonder Comes Glory

Rom. 8:28: All Things—Even Death!

Rom. 8:38–39: No Separation

Rom. 14:7–9: Lord of the Living and of the Dead

Rom. 14:8: It Doesn't Matter!

1 Cor. 3:22: Death Is Your's

1 Cor. 9:24: The Race of Life

1 Cor. 13:12: Face to Face (see Hymn)

1 Cor. 15:26: The Last Enemy

1 Cor. 15:49: What an Image!

1 Cor. 15:54: Death Is Swallowed Up (*Hos. 13:14*)

1 Cor. 15:54–57: Thanks for the Victory

2 Cor. 1:3: God of All Comfort

2 Cor. 3:18: What a Change!

2 Cor. 4:17: Light Affliction, Heavy Glory (The Momentary vs. The Eternal)

2 Cor. 5:1: An Eternal Home

2 Cor. 5:6–8: No Stopping of Life, No Separation from Love, No Sorrow with the Lord

2 Cor. 12:9: His Grace Is Sufficient

Gal. 6:7–8: Reap What You Sow (*Prov. 22:8*)

Eph. 3:15: A Family in Heaven?

Phil. 1:21: A Christian Definition of Death (A Christian Philosophy of Life)

Phil. 1:23: With Christ Is Far Better

Phil. 3:20: Citizen of Heaven—Right Now!

1 Thess. 4:13: Our Hope

1 Thess. 4:17–18: Comfort: Caught in Clouds with Christ

1 Thess. 5:9–10: An Appointment to Life

1 Tim. 3:13: The Purchase of a Good Standing (Deacon)

1 Tim. 4:12: Death of a Young Person Who Lived for Christ (*Dan. 1:8*)

2 Tim. 4:6: Departure Time

2 Tim. 4:7: The Battle, the Race and the Faith

2 Tim. 4:8: A Crown of Righteousness

Heb. 2:9: Taste of Death

Heb. 2:15: Fear of Death

Heb. 4:8: A Better Rest (*Ps. 55:6*)

Heb. 5:7: Saved Out of Death

Heb. 9:27: Divine Appointment. The appointment to die is in Adam and has been fulfilled already by all of us. One consequence of this death is the possibility of physical death. However, we shall not all die physically (*1 Cor. 15:51; 1 Thess. 4:15,17; 5:9*).

Heb. 11:4: Dead, Yet Speaking (*Heb. 9:16–17*)

Heb. 11:16: Heaven, a Better Country

Heb. 12:1: Run the Race

James 4:13–15: Business Interrupted!

James 4:14: What Is Your Life? (*Luke 12:20*)
1 Pet. 1:23: How to Live Forever!
1 John 3:2: When We See Him!
Rev. 1:18: Alive Forevermore
Rev. 7:16: The Land of Neither Nor
Rev. 14:13: Rest of the Righteous
Rev. 21:4: The Land of No More
Rev. 22:5: The Land of No Night
Rev. 22:17: Come, Come, Come!
A Description of the Holy City: No Dirt: *Rev. 21:27;*
   No Darkness: *Rev. 22:5*; No Death: *Rev. 21:4*

Note: I did not include Numbers 23:10 as a funeral text. It reads: "Let me die the death of the righteous, and let my end be like his!" The hireling prophet, Balaam, expressed his desire to share in Israel's blessings. Since he could not curse the Israelites, he could only wish his life's end would resemble that of the righteous men of Israel. From this point of view, the death of a pious Jew was a desirable good (*Keil & Delitzsch*). If defying the will of king Balak issues forth in death, then so be it! says Balaam. But Balaam's wish was not granted (Num. 31:8). You see the importance of studying the context before applying scriptures for funeral texts.

COMMITTAL AT THE GRAVESITE

The committal begins at the signal of the mortician, with the minister standing at the *head* of the grave. Usually at the national cemeteries, the military service comes after the minister has done his part. So also with respect to the ritual performed by fraternal organizations like the Masons. The minister conducts his services first and then gives way to the military or fraternal groups. However, in the church, within the church edifice, the pastor is in charge, and all other groups must precede the Christian church service. Let the last word be the Word, not the ritual of any man-made organization. At the gravesite, once the minister gives the benediction, he should step back, out of the way. Usually, at this point, if there are no other services, the mortician will direct the friends and family to place flowers on the casket, which will then be lowered into the grave. Some undertakers dismiss the family and friends to return to their cars without remaining to watch the casket lowered.

COMMITTAL SCRIPTURES

May be read at the cemetery (Any one passage may suffice. The passages from the Psalms are appropriate for non-Christians as well).

Ps. 39:4–5: Lord, make me to know my end, and what is the measure of my days, that I may know how frail I am. Indeed, You have made my days as handbreadths, and my age is as nothing before You; certainly every man at his best state is but vapor.

Ps. 90:9–12: For all our days have passed away in Your wrath; we finish our years like a sigh. The days of our lives are seventy years; and if by reason of strength they are eighty years, yet their boast is only labor and sorrow; for it is soon cut off, and we fly away. Who knows the power of Your anger? For as the fear of You, so is Your wrath. So teach us to number our days, that we may gain a heart of wisdom.

John 11:25–26: Jesus said to her, "I am the resurrection and the life. He who believes in Me, though he may die, he shall live. And whoever lives and believes in Me shall never die. Do you believe this?"

John 12:24: Most assuredly, I say to you, unless a grain of wheat falls into the ground and dies, it remains alone; but if it dies, it produces much grain.

2 Tim. 4:6–8: For I am already being poured out as a drink offering, and the time of my departure is at hand. I have fought the good fight, I have finished the race, I have kept the faith. Finally, there is laid up for me the crown of righteousness which the Lord, the righteous judge, will give to me on that Day, and not to me only but also to all who have loved His appearing.

Rev. 1:17–18: And when I saw Him, I fell at His feet as dead. But He laid His right hand on me, saying to me, "Do not be afraid; I am the First and the Last. I am He who lives, and was dead, and behold, I am alive forevermore. Amen.

And I have the keys of Hades and of Death."

Rev. 14:13: Then I heard a voice from heaven saying to me,
"Write: 'Blessed are the dead who die in the Lord from
now on'" "Yes" says the Spirit, "that they may rest from
their labors, and their works follow them."

FUNERAL COMMITTAL

*The undertaker stands with flowers, dirt or ashes to be put upon
the casket as the minister speaks:* Forasmuch as it has pleased Almighty God, in His wise providence, to take out of this world
the soul of our deceased (brother, sister, friend, etc.), we therefore commit (his, her) body to the ground: Earth to earth, ashes
to ashes, dust to dust. We look for the life of the world to come,
through our Lord and Savior, Jesus Christ, at whose second coming in glorious majesty, the earth and the sea shall give up their
dead.

The corrupted bodies of those who sleep in Him shall be
changed; and the bodies of those alive remaining shall also be
changed and made like unto His own body of glory. This shall
be done according to the mighty working whereby He is able to
subdue all things unto Himself.

Then I heard a voice from heaven saying to me, "Write:
'Blessed are the dead who die in the Lord from now on.'" "Yes"
says the Spirit, "they may rest from their labors, and their works
follow them."

Prayer: Thank You, Father, for the memory of the deceased,
for all (he, she) meant in the life of the church, in the lives of the

family members and friends. Father, use this moment to draw us closer to Him who loved us and shed His own blood for us. In the days ahead, by Your grace, draw this family and friends closer to each other in love. We look forward to that day when the circle shall never again be broken. In the Name of Jesus Christ we pray.

EULOGY AND COMMITTAL POEMS

Unfold thy bosom, faithful tomb,
Take this new treasure to thy trust;
And give these sacred relics room
To slumber in thy silent dust.—Isaac Watts

Servant of God, well done! Rest from thy loved employ:
The battle fought, the victory won, enter thy Master's joy.
The pains of death are past, labor and sorrow cease,
And life's long warfare closed at last,
Thy soul is found in peace.—*James Montgomery*

Servant of God, well done!
Thy glorious warfare's past;
The battle's fought, the race is won,
And thou art crowned at last.—Charles Wesley

Rejoice for a brother deceased,
    our loss is his infinite gain;
A soul out of prison released,

and freed from its bodily chain;
With songs let us follow his flight,
    and mount with his spirit above,
Escaped to the mansion of light,
    and lodged in the Eden of love.—*Charles Wesley*

The strife is o'er; the battle done. The victory of life is won;
The song of triumph has begun, Hallelujah.

Another soldier's gone to get a great reward;
He's fought the fight and kept the faith,
    and now gone home to God.
He fought until he fell upon the battlefield,
And then he heard the General say,
    "Lay down your sword and shield."
Some day we'll meet again, our loved ones gone before;
Some day we'll reach that happy land, where parting is no
    more.—*B.J. Perkins*

Come, ye disconsolate, where'er ye languish;
    Come to the mercy-seat, fervently kneel;
Here bring your wounded hearts, here tell your anguish;
    Earth has no sorrow that heaven cannot heal.
Joy of the desolate, light of the straying,
    Hope of the penitent, fadeless and pure,
Here speaks the Comforter, tenderly saying,
    Earth has no sorrow that heaven cannot cure.—T. Moore

Rock of Ages, cleft for me, let me hide myself in Thee;
Let the water and the blood, from Thy wounded side which flowed,
Be of sin the double cure, save from wrath and make me pure.

Not the labors of my hands can fulfill Thy law's demands;
Could my zeal no respite know, could my tears forever flow,
All for sin could not atone; Thou must save, and Thou alone.

Nothing in my hand I bring, simply to Thy cross I cling;
Naked, come to Thee for dress, helpless, look to Thee for grace;
Foul, I to the fountain fly, wash me, Savior, or I die!

While I draw this fleeting breath, when mine eyes shall close in
    death,
When I soar to worlds unknown, see Thee on Thy judgment
    throne,
Rock of Ages, cleft for me, let me hide myself in Thee.
                              —*Augustus H. Toplady*

Swift to its close ebbs out life's little day;
Earth's joys grow dim, its glories pass away;
Change and decay in all around I see.
O Thou who changest not, abide with me.

I fear no foe, with Thee at hand to bless;
Ills have no weight, and tears no bitterness.
Where is death's sting? Where, grave, thy victory?
I triumph still, if Thou abide with me.

Hold Thou Thy cross before my closing eyes;
Shine through the gloom and point me to the skies:
Heaven's morning breaks and earth's vain shadows flee;
In life, in death, O Lord, abide with me.——Henry F. Lyte

God Is Able

His tabernacles are amiable — He is to no man answerable — the Table He prepares is delectable — His company is desirable — to Him unrighteousness is detestable — His Word is edible — in Him life is favorable — His plans are feasible — His law is honorable — the riches of His grace are immeasurable — His counsel is immutable — His peace is impassable.

His humanity is impeccable — His armor is impenetrable — His dealings are imperceptible — His stand against evil is implacable — His thoughts are imponderable — with Him nothing shall be impossible — His resources are incalculable — His beauty is incomparable — His crowns are incorruptible — He cures the incurable — His efforts to save are indefatigable.

His ways are indefinable — His entries in the Book of Life are indelible — His majesty is indescribable — His kingdom is indestructible — His Sovereignty is indisputable — His Scriptures are indissoluble — His unity is indivisible — His judgment is inescapable — His proofs are infallible — His mercies are innumerable — His methods are inscrutable.

His love is inseparable — His blood is invaluable — His Spirit is invisible — His Creatorhood is irrefutable — what He breaks down is irreparable — His grace is irresistible.

His deeds are more than notable — all His paths are peaceable — and His doctrine is profitable — His reasons are reasonable — His promises are reliable — every morning His compassions are renewable — His sword is swift and terrible — His decrees are unalterable — His glory is unapproachable — His wisdom is unattainable — In holiness He establishes our hearts unblameable — His priesthood is unchangeable.

His armies are undefeatable—His resurrection is undeniable — His mind is unfathomable — His blessings are unforgettable — His character is unimpeachable — His foundations are unmovable — His fire unquenchable — His integrity is unquestionable — He keeps us unrebukeable — His greatness is unsearchable — His Gift is unspeakable — His truth is unstoppable — what He guards is untouchable — and His performance is unsurpassable. Surely our God is able!

Wm. L. Banks — With my computer and *Random House Dictionary*, I looked up all the words ending with "able" and "ible." Then I sought to connect them with Bible verses. The above is the result.

Homecoming Sermon Texts

Jacob's Return: Obedience to God (Gen. 31:3); Fear of Esau
(Gen. 32:7); Blessed Results (Gen. 33:4)
Ps. 137:1–6: No Song Away from Home
Luke 8:39: Go Back Home, and . . .
Luke 15:11–32: The Prodigal: Bad Experiences (vv. 14–16)
Remembering Home (v. 17); Joy of the Father (vv. 22–24)

Initiative

The story is told of a pastor who left his home each day at a certain hour, returning at exactly the same time every day. Since no one seemed to know where he went or what he was doing, suspicions were aroused, and a committee was appointed to investigate. Following him as he left his home, they were amazed to see him pull up at a railroad track outside of town just as the afternoon flyer screamed by, whistle blowing.

As it disappeared in the distance, he started his motor and headed back toward town. The men were nonplussed. Later, the committee bravely asked the meaning of his action. The pastor with a sly grin replied, "I just enjoy seeing something go that I don't have to push."

Installations

SERVICE FOR CHURCH OFFICERS

Opening Hymn
Scripture
Prayer
Hymn
Welcome
Roll Call of Elected Officers for the New Year*
Charge to the Officers (by the Pastor)
Church Covenant
Prayer of Consecration
Hymn
Presentation of Preacher
Selection
Sermon
Invitation
Offering
Remarks
Closing Hymn
Benediction

---

* The church clerk usually does this. If the list is too long to read, present the names in printed form, or read just those who are presidents or chairmen.

A CHARGE:
INSTALLATION OF OFFICERS FOR THE NEW YEAR #1

Congratulations! On being elected as officers of the _____ church for the year___, the church has committed to you the privilege of leadership and positions of honor. As your pastor, I can appreciate you and all that you mean in the life of the local assembly. I take pleasure therefore in making this charge to you:

Ever be mindful of the sacredness of your task. Be faithful in the discharge of your responsibilities. Work with a holy enthusiasm, not with just-get-by-ism, for that dishonors the Lord. Seek the guidance of the Holy Spirit and bathe all that you do in prayer. And become better students of the Bible, for only then will you have the proper motivation, the correct methods and the spiritual means to accomplish your goal. Above all, look to Jesus Christ, the Head of the church, for He is the One who shed His blood for you and called you out of darkness into His marvelous light. Remember, you are God's workmanship, created in Christ Jesus for good works. God bless you as you embark upon a new year of service for the Master. May it be yours to hear Him say, "Well done!"

"Is your place a small place? Tend it with care! He set you there. Is your place a large place? Guard it with care! He set you there. Whate'er your place, it is not yours alone, but His who set you there."

—John Oxenham

A CHARGE:
INSTALLATION OF OFFICERS FOR THE NEW YEAR #2

Christian Friends and Fellow-Workers:

On being elected as officers of the _____ church for the year_____, the church has committed to you a task as important as it lies within her power to bestow. Yours is a high privilege of guiding and inspiring boys and girls, men and women in the way of eternal life. I trust that you recognize the sacredness of your task and pray that you will approach it with a holy enthusiasm. I charge you, therefore, to be faithful in your service, proficient in your guidance, relying wholly upon the leadership of the Holy Spirit for direction, keeping ever in mind that you are laborers together with God in Christ (1 Cor. 3:9; 2 Cor. 6:1) and that Christ is the Head of the church (Eph. 1:22–23; Col. 1:18).

—Dr. C. R. McCreary

INSTALLATION SERVICE: PASTOR #1

Invocation
Hymn
Scripture
Prayer
Gloria Patri
Selection
Welcome
Response
Introduction of Preacher
Selection
Sermon
Invitation
Offering
Installation: Greeting
                Pulpit Committee Statement*
                Charge to the Church
                Charge to the Pastor
                Presentation of Church Key*
                Presentation of Church Bible
                Presentation of Church Hymnal
                Prayer of Installation
                Presentations to Pastor*
Remarks by the Pastor
Benediction

---

* May be omitted

148

INSTALLATION SERVICE: PASTOR #2

Processional
Call to Worship
Invocation
Welcome
Selection
Greetings
Scripture
Introduction of Preacher
Selection
Sermon
Hymn: Congregational
Offering
Prayer
Installation: Covenant: Chairman of Deacons
            Charge to Pastor
            Charge to Church
            Prayer of Installation
            Presentation of Keys: Chairman of Trustees
Pastoral Response
Hymn
Benediction

INSTALLATION SERVICE: PASTOR #3

Invocation
Hymn
Scripture
Prayer
Hymn
Welcome
Installation: Presentation of Bible
              Presentation of Hymnal
              Charge to Minister
              Charge to Deacons
              Charge to Congregation
              Prayer
Introduction of Preacher
Solo
Sermon
Invitation
Offering
Remarks by Pastor
Hymn
Benediction

INSTALLATION SERVICE: PASTOR #4

Prelude
Processional
Call to Worship
Hymn
Invocation — Chant
Scripture Lesson: Old Testament
                    New Testament
Gloria Patri
Hymn
Litany: Responsive Reading
Solo
Greetings: Representatives
Introduction of Preacher
Anthem
Installation Sermon
Hymn and Invitation
Offering
Presentation of Pastor-Elect by Chairman of Deacons
Prayer of Installation
Charge to the Church
Charge to the Pastor
Remarks: Newly installed Pastor
Closing Hymn
Benediction
Recessional and Postlude

INSTALLATION SERVICE: PASTOR # 5

Call to Worship (Invocation)
Hymn
Old Testament Lesson
Anthem
New Testament Lesson
Hymn
Welcome: Chairman, Deacon Board
Response: Chairman, Visiting Deacon
Anthem
Installation Conducted by Master of Ceremonies
              Charge to Minister
              Charge to Church
Prayer
Introduction of Preacher
Hymn
Sermon
Offering and Dedication
Remarks   Inducted Minister
Remarks   Moderator of Association
Hymn
Benediction

INSTALLATION SERVICE: PASTOR #6

Procession
Invocation
Opening Hymn
Scripture: Old Testament
              New Testament
Welcome Address
Response
Solo
Introduction of Preacher
Selection: Choir
Sermon
Dedicatory Hymn
Covenant of Dedication
Presentation of Bible
Presentation of Hymnal
Charge to the Deacons
Charge to the Trustees
Charge to the Church Auxiliaries
Charge to the Congregation
Installation Prayer
Declaration of Installation
Hymn of Consecration
Offering
Remarks: Pastor
Benediction and Postlude

Junior Church

Some churches have established what is called a "Junior Church," composed of young people up to age sixteen or thereabouts. They have a separate auditorium, a separate service, and the message is brought by one of the associate ministers. Some assemblies even have a separate Lord's Supper service on their Communion Sunday. There is no scriptural basis for a "Junior Church." In fact, harm is done when the generation gap is fostered.

How much better it is to have young and old together in the worship service, mutually helping and sharing with one another. Although nurseries are very practical, all who are capable of understanding what is spoken should be together. Such a mixture may tax the preacher's ability to communicate effectively, but the Holy Spirit is able. It is possible to preach in such a way that all age groups seated together are edified.

Library, The Pastor's

Basic working tools include: (1) Bibles (2) Dictionaries (3) Concordances (4) Hymnals (5) Theology books (6) Commentaries (7) Encyclopedia (8) Lexicons. Every pastor should have these books at hand.

1. *Bibles:* My primary Bibles are the *New Scofield Reference Bible* (New King James Version). *The Nelson Study Bible* is extremely helpful. Other versions, translations and paraphrases in my library are: *New American Standard*; *Amplified*, *Today's English Version* (Good News), Living Bible, Moffatt, JB Phillips (NT), Montgomery, *New International* (NIV), *Revised Standard Version* (RSV), *New English Bible* (NEB), *New World Translation* (Watchtower Society: Jehovah's Witnesses). I have also the *Thompson Chain Reference*, and the Pilgrim Edition. There are others available, such as Ryrie, Zodhiates, etc.

2. *Dictionaries: The American Heritage Dictionary*; the *World Book Dictionary*. And on CDRom, *Random House*.

3. *Concordances: Strong's Exhaustive Concordance*; *Young's Analytical Concordance* are **musts!** *Judson's Concordance to Hymns* is helpful.

4. *Hymnals: The New National Baptist Hymnal*; the *Baptist Standard Hymnal*; *His Fullness Songs* (Church of Christ Holiness, U.S.A); *Gospel Pearls*; *Hymns for the Living Church*;

Christian Praise; *Tabernacle Hymns*; *Sing His Praise*—these are some of the fourteen hymnals I have.

5. *Theology Books: Systematic Theology* by Lewis Sperry Chafer of Dallas Seminary; *Lectures in Systematic Theology* by H.C. Thiessen; *Systematic Theology* by Louis Berkhof.

6. *Commentaries:* <u>Old Testament</u>: Keil and Delitzsch. Psalms: *Treasury of David* by Spurgeon is invaluable. <u>New Testament</u>: *Romans* by Donald Grey Barnhouse; *John* by Leon Morris. Lenski's set is very helpful with Greek grammar, but is nondispensational, amillennial. As for one-volume complete Bible commentaries: *Wycliffe* (Moody Press); *New Bible Commentary* (Eerdmans). *Believer's Commentary* by Wm. MacDonald. I own the very liberal *International Critical Commentary* (ICC). The *New International Commentary* is conservative. On my laptop computer I have (1) *Hermeneutika* (2) *PC Study Bible* (3) *Bibliotheca Sacra* (4) *Online Bible*.

7. *Encyclopedia:* I have the *World Book Encyclopedia*. Also *Encyclopaedia Britannica* on CD. Every pastor should own a set of *The International Standard Bible Encyclopedia* (ISBE).

8. *Lexicons:* For those of you who still work with the original languages, you know the value of Brown, Driver, Briggs' *Hebrew Lexicon*; and of Thayer's *Greek Lexicon*, as well as Arndt & Gingrich's *Lexicon*; and the *Analytical Greek Lexicon*.

9. *Miscellaneous:* Girdlestone's *Synonyms of the OT*; Trench's *Synonyms of the NT*; the latest World Almanac is very valuable; Kittel's *Theological Dictionary of the NT*; *Westminster Historical Atlas to the Bible*.

Litigation

Churches in court violate the Scriptures and disregard our stand on separation of church and state. We live in a litigious age. What can be done about the plague of saints suing saints? Here are some suggestions:

1. Prayer is always necessary and valuable.
2. Bible Study: Thoroughly teach 1 Corinthians 6:1–8 and Ephesians 4:31–32. Study Matthew 18:15–17 and make it a part of the provision for handling grievances.
3. Strengthen the church Constitution/Bylaws so that they provide for handling conflict. The judge will require the plaintiff to follow that procedure.
4. Be above board in all financial dealings. Congregations have a right to know how much money comes in and how every penny is spent.
5. Pastors and church officers may benefit by attending Conflict and Group Dynamics classes, offered by seminaries and other church and parachurch organizations.
6. Utilize the Reconciliation Board established by the local association to which the church voluntarily belongs (voted on by the church and a matter of record). If the parties

involved agree beforehand to binding arbitration, the Court will hold valid the decision made by the Reconciliation Board.

7. Live a clean life!

Marriage

THE WEDDING CEREMONY # 1

Salutation

All participants present reverently stand before the minister who shall say: "Our help is in the name of the Lord, who made heaven and earth. Except the Lord build the house, they labor in vain that build it."

Address

Dearly beloved, we are gathered here in the presence of God to join this man and this woman in holy marriage; which is instituted of God, regulated by His commandments, blessed by our Lord Jesus Christ and to be held in honor among all men. Let us therefore reverently remember that God has established and sanctified marriage for the welfare and happiness of mankind.

Our Savior has declared that a man shall forsake his father and mother and cleave unto his wife. By His apostles, He has instructed those who enter into this relation to cherish a mutual esteem and love; to bear with each other's infirmities and weaknesses; to comfort each other in sickness, trouble and sorrow; in honesty and industry to provide for each other and for their household in temporal things; to pray for and encourage each other in the things which pertain to God; and to live together as the heirs of the grace of life.

Forasmuch as these two persons have come hither to be made one in this holy estate, if there be any here present who knows any just cause why they may not lawfully be joined in marriage, I require him now to make it known or ever after to hold his peace.

Charge

The minister shall then charge the persons who are to be married as follows: I charge you both, before the great God the Searcher of all hearts, that if either of you know any impediment why you may not lawfully be joined together in marriage, you do now confess it. For be you well assured that if any persons are joined together otherwise than as God's Word allows, their union is not blessed by Him.

Prayer

Vows

Then the minister shall say to the man:

_____, will you have this woman to be your wife, and will you pledge your faith to her, in all love and honor, in all duty and service, in all faith and tenderness, to live with her and cherish her, according to the ordinance of God, in the holy bond of marriage?

The man: I will.

Then the minister shall say to the woman:

_____, will you have this man to be your husband, and will you pledge your faith to him, in all love and honor, in all duty and service, in all faith and tenderness, to live with him and cherish him, according to the ordinance of God, in the holy bond of marriage?

The woman: I will.

Then the minister may say:

Who gives this woman to be married to this man?

Then the father (or guardian, or any friend) of the woman shall put her right hand into the hand of the minister, who shall cause the man with his right hand to take the woman by her right hand and to say after him:

I, _____, take you,_____, to be my wedded wife; and I do promise and covenant, before God and these witnesses, to be your loving and faithful husband, in plenty and in want, in joy and in sorrow, in sickness and in health, as long as we both shall live.

Then shall they loose hands; and the woman with her right hand taking the man by his right hand, shall likewise say after the minister:

I, _____, take you,_____, to be my wedded husband; and I do promise and covenant, before God and these witnesses, to be your loving and faithful wife, in plenty and in want, in joy and in sorrow, in sickness and in health, so long as we both shall live.

Presentation of the Ring

The ring shall be given to the minister, who shall return it to the man, who shall then put it upon the fourth finger of the woman's left hand, saying after the minister:

I give you this ring in token and pledge of our constant faith and abiding love.

Prayer

Declaration

Then shall the minister say unto all present:

By the authority committed unto me as a minister of the church of Christ, I declare that_____and_____are now husband and wife, according to the ordinance of God and the law of the state: in the name of the Father, and of the Son, and of the Holy Spirit. Amen.

Then, causing the husband and wife to join their right hands, the minister shall say: What therefore God has joined together, let no man put asunder.

Benediction

Adapted: Order for the Solemnization of Marriage in *The Book of Common Worship*, copyrighted by the Presbyterian Board of Publication, 1906, and is used with their permission.

THE WEDDING CEREMONY # 2

The minister faces the man on the minister's left, the woman on the groom's left stands facing the minister on the minister's right. The minister then speaks:
Dearly beloved: We are gathered together here in the sight of God, and in the face of this company, to join together this man and this woman in holy matrimony, instituted of God, which is commended of the apostle Paul to be honorable among all men. It is therefore not by any to be entered into unadvisedly or lightly; but reverently, discreetly, advisedly and in the fear of God. Into this holy estate, these two persons present come now to be joined. If any man can show just cause why they may not lawfully be joined together, let him now speak or else hereafter forever hold his peace.

The minister pauses momentarily, then speaks to the couple: I require and charge you both, that if either of you know any impediment why you may not be lawfully joined together in matrimony, you do now confess it.

If no impediment is alleged, the minister says to the man: Will you have this woman to your wedded wife, to live together after God's ordinance, in the holy estate of matrimony? Will you love her, comfort her, honor and keep her, in sickness and in health; and, forsaking all others, keep you only unto her, so long as you both shall live?

After the man answers "I will," the minister says to the woman:

Will you have this man to your wedded husband, to live together after God's ordinance, in the holy estate of matrimony? Will you obey him and serve him, love, honor and keep him, in sickness and in health; and, forsaking all others, keep you only unto him, so long as you both shall live?

After the woman answers "I will," the minister says:

Who gives this woman to be married to his man?

The father or person giving the woman in marriage then steps back and is seated. Receiving the woman at her father's or friend's hands, the minister shall cause the man with his right hand to take the woman by her right hand, and to say after him as follows:

I, _____, take you,_____, to be my wedded wife, to have and to hold from this day forward, for better for worse, for richer for poorer, in sickness and in health, to love and to cherish, till death us do part, according to God's holy ordinance; and thereto I pledge you my faith.

The man and woman loose hands. Then the woman, with her right hand taking the man by his right hand, shall likewise repeat after the minister:

I, _____, take you,_____, to be my wedded husband, to have and to hold from this day forward, for better for worse, for richer for poorer, in sickness and in health, to love, cherish and to obey, till death us do part, according to God's holy ordinance; and thereto I give you my faith.

They again loose their hands. The best man gives the ring to the minister who in turn gives it to the groom, who shall give it to the woman. He shall place it upon the fourth finger of the woman's left hand. And the man, holding the ring there, shall repeat after the minister:

As a pledge and in token of the vows between us made, with this ring I thee wed. In the Name of the Father, and of the Son, and of the Holy Spirit. Amen.

If a double ring ceremony, the minister receives the ring from the maid of honor, gives it to the bride and repeats the above with the woman holding the ring on the man's finger.

After the pledging of the ring, the minister joins their right hands together, and shall say: That which God has joined together, let no man put asunder.

Speaking to the company gathered together to witness the ceremony, the minister shall say: Forasmuch as _____(man) and _____ (woman) have consented together in holy wedlock, and have witnessed the same before God and this company, and thereto have given and pledged their faith, each to the other, and have declared the same by giving and receiving a ring (rings), and by joining hands, I pronounce that they are man and wife, in the name of the Father, and of the Son the Lord Jesus Christ, and of the Holy Spirit. Amen.

There may be a solo at this point.

The bride and groom may kneel or remain standing as the minister prays. At the end of the prayer, the minister bids the groom to salute (kiss) the bride. The bridal party then leaves.

WEDDING ORDER # 1

Some suggestions: Make sure you ask what selections are to be sung. Failure to inquire and give approval may prove embarrassing, for some music sung at church weddings is inappropriate. Concerning photographers: Some ministers regard picture-taking during the ceremony distracting, even irreverent, and find it necessary to announce beforehand that: (1) No pictures are to be taken *during* the ceremony, or (2) Only the official, professional photographer will be allowed to take pictures *during* the ceremony.

Preliminary

1. Music: Organ recital, vocal numbers
2. Escort Groom's parents (right side of auditorium)
3. Escort Bride's mother (left side of auditorium)

Processional

1. Minister, Groom, Best Man
2. Bridesmaids and Ushers
3. Maid of Honor or Matron of Honor
4. Ring Bearer
5. Flower Girl
6. Bride and Father (or near Relative)

Ceremony

1. Address to Congregation
2. Giving away of the Bride
3. Address to Groom and Bride
4. Song
5. Vows

6. Ring Ceremony
7. Blessing
8. Song
9. Finalize Vows
10. Salute the Bride

Recessional

WEDDING ORDER # 2

Special Music
1. Seating of the Family
2. Minister, Groom, Best Man
3. Groomsmen, Ring Bearer
4. Maid of Honor
5. Bridesmaids, Flower Girl
6. Rolling of the Carpet
7. Bride and Father (or the one giving her away)
8. Prayer
9. Scripture: Gen. 2:18–24; Eph. 5:22–33
10. A Charge to the Couple
11. Solo
12. Vows, Exchanging of Rings
13. Prayer
14. Solo—The Lord's Prayer
15. Pronouncement of Marriage; Bridal Salute
16. Recessional

WEDDING ARRANGEMENT

Leave
Enter

Usher — Bridesmaid

Usher — (Bride's Father) — Bridesmaid

Usher — Bridesmaid

Best Man — Maid (Matron) of Honor

Ring Bearer — Flower Girl

Groom — Bride

Minister

At a given point in the ceremony, the bride's father (or whoever "gives her away") takes his seat. The pastor should have a general idea of this standard arrangement. Although usually someone else acts as the consultant for the arrangement and procedure, it helps for the minister to know this basic operation and arrangement.

REAFFIRMATION OF MARRIAGE VOWS:
GOLDEN ANNIVERSARY

We are gathered together here in the sight of God, and in the face of this company, to reaffirm the vows made fifty years ago between these two precious saints,_____and_____. God has blessed them with long life, a reasonable portion of health and tremendous growth in grace. Through the years their love for Jesus Christ has grown and expressed itself in their love for each other. And we are delighted to be witnesses of such Holy Spirit-empowered stability and to share in this festive occasion that surely redounds to the glory of the Lord Jesus Christ.

Husband: Will you reaffirm before God and these witnesses to continue to be a true and devoted husband, true to_____ in sickness and in health, in joy and sorrow, in prosperity and in adversity; and that forsaking all others you will keep yourself to her, and to her only, so long as you both shall live?

Wife: Do you promise before God and this company that you will continue to be to_____a true and devoted wife, to obey him and serve him, love, honor and keep him, in sickness and in health; and, forsaking all others, keep yourself to him, so long as you both shall live?

Congregation: Will all of you witnessing these promises do all in your power to uphold these two persons in love, prayer and devotion? If so, please answer, "We will."

Husband and Wife hold hands.

Husband: I, _____, do reaffirm to you,_____,from this day

forward, for better for worse, for richer for poorer, in sickness and in health, to love and to cherish, until we are parted by death; as God is my witness, I give you my promise.

Wife: I, _____, do reaffirm to you, _____, from this day forward, for better for worse, for richer for poorer, in sickness and in health, to love, cherish and to obey, until we are parted by death; as God is my witness, I give you my promise.

Exchange of Ring(s): I give you this ring, as a symbol of my vow, and with all that I am, and all that I have, I honor you; in the name of the Father, and of the Son, and of the Holy Spirit. Amen.

Prayer

Pronouncement:

Now that _____ and _____ have recommitted themselves to each other by solemn vows before God as witness and before us as witnesses, and have shown their affection, trust and love for one another by giving and receiving of a ring (or rings) and by joining hands, it is my happy privilege to announce that these two saints, pronounced man and wife fifty years ago, are still man and wife. What God has wrought no man shall put asunder. May Jesus Christ be praised!

Men's Day:
Sermon Texts

Josh. 6:1–5, 27: The Christian Soldier: God Calls Soldiers; God Chooses Strategy; God Conquers Strongholds

Judg. 16:28: A Men's Day Sermon for Strong Men

1 Sam. 13:14: A Man After the Heart of God (*Ps. 89:20; Acts 13:22*)

2 Sam. 10:12: Play the Man! (KJV)

1 Chron. 12:32: A Man for the Times

2 Chron. 18:7: There Is Yet One Man!

Ps. 12:1: Faithful Men (Wm. MacDonald)

Ps. 84:11: Profile of an Upright Man

Prov. 27:18: The Man Who Waits on His Master

Mal. 4:6: Father's Day

Matt. 13:55: (Carpenter); *Mark 3:21*: (Crazy); *Matt. 27:63:* (Con-man): Who Is This Christ?

Mark 4:41: What Manner of Man Is This?

Luke 2:25: A Man Who Was Ready

Acts 6:3: The Kind of Men God Needs (F.W. Dixon)

Acts 11:24: Righteous Barnabas: Fullness, Faith, Fruit

Acts 15:26: Men Who Live Dangerously

Rom. 6:6: Our Old Man; Description, Deliverance and Destruction

1 Cor. 16:13: Quit You Like Men! (KJV)
1 Thess. 2:10–12: Exhorted, Encouraged, Entreated
1 John 3:11–14: Brotherly Love: Murder, Mastermind,
   Motive, Message

Miscellaneous Occasions: Sermon Texts

Cornerstone Laying:

Hag. 1:3–8; 2:4–9: The House of the Lord of Hosts
1 Kings 6:7: God's Way to Build God's House
Ps. 118:22–23: The Chief Cornerstone
Matt. 16:18: A Sure Foundation (*1 Cor. 3:9–11*)

Deacons:

1 Tim. 3:13: A Good Standing and Great Boldness

Dedications:

Gen. 28:17–19: Bethel, God's House
Ps. 84:1–4: Sparrows and Swallows
Ps. 122:1–9: Peace, Prosperity in This Place

Groundbreaking:

1 Chron. 22:19: The House to Be Built
2 Chron. 2:1–6: A Great House for a Great God
Ps. 127:1: The House that God Builds
Isa. 58:12: The Breach Repairers (W.H.R. Powell)

Missions:

Isa. 6:9: To Tell or Not to Tell (*Jer. 35:13; 2 Sam. 1:20*)
Acts 1:8: Divine Imperative, Devilish Impediments, Delightful Incentive
Acts 1:11; 2 Pet. 3:8: Missions and the Second Coming
Acts 26:18: Paul's Purpose in Preaching
Rom. 10:15: Beautiful Feet (*Isa. 52:7*)

Mortgage Burning:

1 Cor. 6:20, 7:23: Bought and Paid For

Pastor's Aid:

1 Cor. 9:14: Helping to Fulfill God's Ordination
Gal. 6:6: No Communication Gap
1 Tim. 5:17: Double Pay

Thanksgiving Day:

Ezra 8:21: A Straight Way Before Our God (KJV)
Matt. 6:19–21: Treasures

Trustees:

1 Cor. 4:2: Faithful Stewards

Ushers:

Ps. 84:10: The Days of the Divine Doorkeeper

Women's Day:

Prov. 31:10: Search for a Gem
Acts 9:36–43: Dorcas, A Woman of Wonderful Works
Acts 16:14–15: Lydia: Busy, Baptized, Believer, Beggar
Heb. 11:11: Portrait of a Princess
1 Pet. 3:1–7: Daughters of Sarah
1 Pet. 3:1–7: Adornment, Apparel, Array: God's Fashion Show

Missions

We have observed that far too many churches do not have or have never had an Annual Missions Conference. Surely our Lord would be pleased if more of our pastors would consider starting such a conference. There are several approaches and numerous suggestions for increased missions contributions and awareness. In my first pastorate we tried the Faith Promise approach. Having established a list of missions boards that the members expressed an interest in supporting, and which were acceptable to the pastor, pledge cards and envelopes were distributed to the membership. The card read:

MY FAITH PROMISE CARD

In dependence upon God I will endeavor to give EACH MONTH toward worldwide missionary work the following amount: $ _____

NAME _____ ADDRESS _____

ENVELOPE No. _____

"Every man according as he purposeth in his heart, so let him give" (2 Cor. 9:7).

The contributors then checked off the mission board he or she desired to receive the contribution for that month.

In my second pastorate we simply split the envelopes, one side for the general offering, the other side for missions. Members were informed that all missions money collected through the envelope system would go to a particular board. Our Sunday School and Missionary Society contributed to other missions. To encourage giving, a missions conference was held annually for at least three days. Friday usually began with a film; on Saturday, missionary speakers, question and answer period, invitation, challenge and refreshments.

On Sunday morning we sought to have the executive secretary of the Foreign Mission Board, or a missionary brother on furlough, or the pastor to preach. In the afternoon a dinner was served, and again a missionary would close out the evening service. During the conference display booths were maintained.

One key to a successful missions conference is to get the entire congregation involved, not just the Missionary Society. Forming a Junior Missionary Society was helpful. Other churches were invited. All the money raised was given to the participating missionaries. It is not the purpose of mission clubs and church auxiliaries to use the missions conference to raise money for the church. Money given during the missions conference goes to the missionaries!

Work without vision is mercenary;
Vision without work is visionary;
But work and vision is Missionary.
—Author unknown

Morning Worship Service

GENERAL COMMENTS

Some churches have their announcements, offerings, recognition of visitors, etc., after the sermon. This is not the ideal. In the examples given of morning services, I have sought to encourage pastors to put the sermon near the end of the service. Hopefully, the congregation will leave with the message still burning within their hearts. Breaks in the flow of the worship service, especially long announcement periods, may be devastating. They make it difficult to get back into the flow.

Some ministers remain in their studies until preaching time. There is some value in this if the pastor spends such time in prayer. It would benefit more, however, after earlier prayer, to sit in the auditorium, catch the drift of the service, sense the spiritual mood, see and be seen, get an idea of who sits where, be inspired by the physical presence of the singing groups, etc.

In some churches the services are spoiled by having too many offerings! Certainly the regular or general offering should be taken before the sermon. Customarily, if it is a guest preacher, a love offering is taken afterwards. Some churches lift the speaker's love gift before he preaches. Others have a set honorarium already budgeted and lift no offering. Whatever the policy or procedure, the guest preacher should be informed beforehand.

One other matter! *No music* is to be played during the prayers! It is distracting and sometimes makes it difficult to hear what is said. It is important that we hear the words of the prayer. May I also discourage the practice of having musicians play the organ while the pastor preaches. That may be the pastor's prerogative and desire, but not necessarily that of the guest preacher!

To me it smacks too much of the musician attempting to orchestrate the service. God's Word does not need this kind of help. It detracts from the message by turning the spotlight on the method of delivery. This should be avoided at all costs. It is the message that is most important!

ORDER OF SERVICE # 1: MORNING

Organ Prelude
*Opening Hymn (May be a processional)
*Call to Worship
*Invocation
*Lord's Prayer (in unison)
Anthem or Hymn
Responsive Reading
*Gloria Patri
Scripture Lesson
Hymn
Pastoral Prayer
Announcements
Offering
Offertory Prayer
*Hymn (Anthem or organ meditation)
Sermon
Invitation
*Hymn
Benediction
Organ Postlude

---

* Stand

ORDER OF SERVICE #2: MORNING

Devotional Period Led by Deacons
Prelude
*Choral Introit
*Call to Worship
*Processional Hymn
*Prayer
*Doxology
Hymn—Congregational
Scripture—Responsive Reading
*Gloria Patri
Prayer
Choral Response
Selection
Announcements
Offering
Welcome to Visitors
*Hymn—Congregational
Selection
Sermon
*Invitation
Prayer of Supplication
Benediction
Meditation
Postlude

---

* Stand

ORDER OF SERVICE # 3: MORNING

Organ Prelude
*Call to Worship
*Invocation
*Lord's Prayer (unison)
Hymn
Responsive Reading
*Gloria Patri
Scripture Lesson
Hymn
Prayer
Announcements
Offertory: Sentences
Offering
Music
Prayer
Hymn
Sermon
*Invitation
*Prayer and Benediction
Organ Postlude

---

* Stand

ORDER OF SERVICE # 4: MORNING

Prelude
The Service of Praise
*Processional Hymn
*Call to Worship
*Invocation
The Service of Prayer
Pastor's Paragraph
Scriptures
*Gloria Patri
Morning Prayer
The Service of Proclamation
Anthem or Hymn
Morning Offering
Anthem
Sermon
The Service of Profession
*Hymn of Dedication
Reception of New Members
Benediction
Postlude

---

* Stand

ORDER OF SERVICE # 5: MORNING

Organ Prelude
*Choral Introit
*Hymn of Praise
Scripture Lesson
Lord's Prayer
Anthem
Recognition of Visitors
Offering
·Meditation and Altar Call
Sermon
Invitation
Presentation of New Members
Closing Hymn
Benediction and Choral Amen
Postlude

_____

* Stand

ORDER OF SERVICE # 6: MORNING

Prelude
*Call to Worship
*Hymn of Praise
*Invocation
Hymn of Devotion
Welcome to Guests
Scripture—Responsive Reading
Pastoral Prayer
Anthem or Special Music
Offertory: Sentences
Music
Offering
Prayer
*Hymn of Affirmation
Sermon
*Hymn of Dedication
Reception of New Members
*Benediction
Postlude

---

* Stand

Mother's Day: Sermon Texts

———

Deut. 5:16: The Honor Due Her
1 Sam. 1:27–28: Hannah's Prayer, Petition, Promise
2 Kings 4:30: Reverence: The Woman's Perception
    Reward: The Prophet's Prediction
    Restoration: A Mother's Perseverance
Isa. 49:15–16: When Mother Forgets (God Is Good)
Isa. 66:13: A Mother's Comfort
Matt. 10:37 (Luke 14:26):
    1. Leave Her (*Gen. 2:24; Mark 10:7; Eph. 5:31*)
    2. Honor Her (*Exod. 20:12; Eph. 6:2*)
    3. Forsake Her Not (*Prov. 1:8, 6:20*)
    4. Do Not Dishonor Her (*Deut. 27:16*)
        — by stealing (*Prov. 28:24*)
        — by cursing (*Exod. 21:17; Prov. 20:20*)
        — by hitting (*Exod. 21:15*)
    5. Obey Her (*Deut. 21:18–19*)
    6. Despise Her Not (*Prov. 15:20, 23:22, 30:17*)
    7. Love Jesus Christ More (*Matt. 10:37; Luke 14:26*)
2 Tim. 1:3–5: Thank God for Mom and Grandmom!

New Year's Day: Watchnight Sermon Texts

Deut. 6:23: Brought Out to Be Brought In

Deut. 11:12: Beginning to the End

Deut. 31:6: No Fear, No Failure, No Forsaking

Josh. 1:2: Arise, Cross Over!

Josh. 1:9: Life Is a Journey

Josh. 3:4: Facing the Unknown

Josh. 13:1: Not Finished Yet!

Ps. 65:11: A Year Provided with Plenty

Ps. 102:24–27: The God Who Changes Not

Ps. 107:2: A New Year's Resolution: The Loud Minority

Ps. 119:126: It's Time for the Lord

Prov. 16:9: Direction for the Year

Prov. 27:1: Man's Ignorance of the Future (*James 4:14*)

Isa. 21:11–12: What Time Is It?

Isa. 40:31: Wait on the Lord

Isa. 43:19: A New Thing in a New Year

Isa. 52:12: Security: From Yesterday, For Tomorrow, For Today (W. Chambers)

Jer. 10:23: What Steps Shall We Take?

Lam. 3:22–23: New Mornings in the New Year

Lam. 3:40: Self-Examination Time

Hos. 10:12: It's Time (*Ps. 119:126*)

Amos 7:7–9: God's Measurement (The Plumb Line)

Matt. 6:33: A New Priority

Matt. 26:27–28: A New Covenant

Luke 12:40: Ready or Not, Here I Come

Luke 17:32: Remember Lot's Wife: Perspective, Perseverance, Preparedness

Acts 2:40: Save Yourself!

Acts 9:6: Turning Point (*Exod. 3:1–6; Matt. 4:18–22*)

Acts 16:25: The Midnight Hour

Rom. 13:11–12: It's Later Than You Think

1 Cor. 7:29, 31: The Time Is Short

2 Cor. 4:16: Resolutions or Renewal?

2 Cor. 10:12: Unchanging Yardstick

Eph. 5:16: Redeem the Time (*Col. 4:5*)

Phil. 3:13–14: Pressing On!

Phil. 4:11–12: Live and Learn

1 Pet. 3:10–11: Resolution: Control Speech, Conduct Self and Chase Serenity

3 John 2: A Prosperous New Year

Rev. 4:11: What Are We Here For? (Purpose of Life)

Rev. 21:5–6: All Things New

Ordination Services

ORDINATION SERVICE # 1: DEACONS*

Invocation
Opening Hymn
Scripture (Deacon)**
Prayer (Deacon)
Hymn
Introduction of Preacher
Musical Selection
Sermon
Invitation
Offering
Ordination: Presentation of Hymnal
            Presentation of Bible
            Charge to Deacon(s)
            Prayer (Hands laid on Candidate)
Hymn
Remarks: Chairman of Deacon Board
          Pastor
Benediction

---

* Some pastors have difficulty using the word "ordination" with respect to deacons. There are men who feel they are deacons for life because they were ordained. Some pastors prefer the word "installation," believing "ordination" should be used for ministers only.
** Acts 6:1–7, 1 Timothy 3:8–13, Psalm 1, etc.

ORDINATION SERVICE #2: DEACONS

Call to Worship
Hymn
Invocation
Scripture
Anthem or other Special Music
Hymn
Sermon
Invitation
Offering
Ordination: Charge to Deacon(s)
               Ordination Prayer
               Laying on of Hands
               Charge to the Church
Hymn
Benediction
Hand of Fellowship by the Congregation

---

* This ordination service courtesy of *Church Administration*, Feb '92, Sunday School Board, SBC

ORDINATION SERVICE #3: DEACONS

Welcome and Announcements
Prelude
Call to Worship
Invocation
Hymn of Praise
Offertory Prayer
Offering
Recognition of Candidates for Ordination (and their families)
Charge to Candidates (and their families)
Charge to the Church
Special Music
Ordination Sermon
Laying on of Hands
Prayer of Dedication
Presentation of Ordination Certificates and Gifts
Hymn of Commitment
Benediction
Response and Postlude

ORDINATION COUNCIL: MINISTERS

The church to which the licensed preacher belongs calls the council in order to examine the candidate's fitness for the gospel ministry. It makes the request fully satisfied that the candidate's conversion, calling and conduct are of Christ. Such councils are usually composed of ministers (and laymen) from other churches or members of an association. In organizing itself, the council elects a moderator or chairman, a secretary or clerk and a cat- echizer, the person who leads in the examination of the candidate.

Examination of the candidate should include an evaluation of his (1) conversion; (2) call to preach; (3) Christian experience in general; (4) education and training; (5) doctrine: Bible, cre- ation, God, Christ, Holy Spirit, Satan, angels, grace, future events, hell, heaven; (6) views concerning the church: Baptist distinctives, civil government, separation, etc. Do not allow the examination to degenerate into a debate between individuals on the council.

When the questioning is over and the council is satisfied with the examination, the candidate should be dismissed. After prayer and discussion the council may then recommend: (1) ordination, or (2) deferment for a stated period so the candidate may become better qualified and prepared, or (3) rejection.

The candidate is called back to the council and notified of the decision. If the majority of the ordained ministers approve of ordination for the candidate, the secretary then delivers a written notice to the church concerning the council's decision. Then if the church accepts the recommendation of the council, the church will vote authorizing the ordination of the candidate.

Churches are warned: Do not set a time for the ordination service until a report is received from the council. Some churches desire the ordination service to be held immediately after the council, thus putting pressure on the council to approve the candidate. This should not be. Do not assume the council will make such a recommendation. But once ordination is approved, then plans may be made for the ordination service.

Ordination Council: Outline of Service

Hymn
Prayer
Nomination and Election of Temporary Moderator
Nomination and Election of Temporary Clerk
Clerk: Read letter from Church calling Pastor
     Read letter inviting Council
     Roll Call
Nomination and Election of Permanent Moderator
Nomination and Election of Permanent Clerk
Introduce Candidate
Inform Council of Purpose
Prayer
Distribute Candidate's position paper
Examination — Questioning (led by Moderator)
     1. Conversion   2. Call

Council considers Conversion and Call: Vote (private)
Motion to proceed with the matter of Doctrine: Vote
    3. Doctrine
Entertain motion Examination be terminated
Ask Candidate to withdraw (or Council withdraws)
Council Considers Doctrine: Vote (private)
1. Recommend church proceed with plans for public ordination.
2. Or satisfied with conversion and call, but due to candidate's inadequate preparation, recommend further studies and reconvene at some later date.
3. Or recommend church not proceed with ordination, and tell why.

Call Candidate in (or Council returns)
Announce Recommendation; thank church for hospitality
Announce Ordination Service Date (if so recommended)
Motion to Adjourn
Prayer for Lord's direction in Candidate's life

Note: Council members sign certificate (if ordination is recommended). Gifts to Council members.

ORDINATION SERVICE #1: MINISTER

Organ Prelude
Hymn
Statement of the Council (by the Moderator or Clerk)
Invocation
Prayer
Anthem or Solo
Scripture Lesson
Sermon
Offering
Prayer of Ordination
Hymn, Anthem or Solo
Charge to the Candidate
Charge to the Church*
Right Hand of Fellowship
Hymn
Benediction

---

* If not being installed as pastor, charge to the church may be omitted.

ORDINATION SERVICE #2: MINISTER

Invocation
Hymn
Scriptures
Prayer
Hymn
Words of Welcome
Introduction of Preacher
Hymn
Sermon
Invitation
Offering
Ordination: Prayer (Hands laid on Candidate)
                Charge to the Candidate
                Charge to the Church
                Right Hand of Fellowship
Hymn
Remarks
Benediction

ORDINATION SERVICE # 3: MINISTER

Call to Worship
Hymn
Invocation
Introductory Statement
Scriptures
Hymn
Sermon
Charge to Candidate
Ordination Prayer
Laying on of Hands
Charge to Church
Presentation of Bible
Hymn
Benediction
Right Hand of Fellowship

ORDINATIONS AND INSTALLATIONS OF MINISTERS: SCRIPTURES

The following scriptures are appropriate for ordinations and installations of ministers. Use one or more of the following:

Numbers 27:15–23
Jeremiah 3:15
Matthew 9:35–38
Matthew 28:18–20
Luke 4:16–22
John 10:1–11
John 21:15–17
Ephesians 4:1–8, 11–13
2 Timothy 4:1–8

Pastoral Anniversary, Installation: Sermon Texts

Exod. 34:34: Moses Went In . . . and Came out

Num. 27:15–17: Joshua: God's Man to Lead God's People Out and to Bring Them In

Ps. 78:72: A Shepherd Who Feeds and Leads

Isa. 52:7: Beautiful Feet (*Rom. 10:15*)

Jer. 3:15: Pastors: God's Gift

Ezek. 2:5: There's a Preacher in Town (*Ezek. 33:33*)

Amos 7:10–17: An Enemy of the Preacher

Luke 9:57–62: Count the Cost (*Matt. 8:18–22*)

Acts 6:2, 4: Fitting and Faithful

Acts 20:28: The Holy Spirit: Places in Authority, Gives the Ability, Holds Accountable

Acts 20:28: Placed, Purpose, Purchased, Price

1 Cor. 16:9: Decision, Door, Devil, Determination

2 Cor. 4:5: Whom We Preach (*Col. 1:28*)

Col. 4:17: Take Heed to Your Ministry (Pray, Preach, Please God)

1 Tim. 6:13–14: A Charge to Keep (Moffatt: "I charge you to keep your commission free from stain, free from reproach, till the appearance of our Lord Jesus Christ.")

2 Tim. 4:2: Preach the Word!

1 Pet. 5:2: Feed the Flock!

Poems

Trust in Him, ye saints, forever;
He is faithful changing never,
Neither force nor guile can sever
Those He loves from Him.
    Keep us, Lord, O keep us cleaving
    To Thyself and still believing
    Till the hour of our receiving
    Promised joys with Thee.
Then we shall be where we would be,
Then we shall be what we should be,
Things that are not now, nor could be,
Soon shall be our own.—*Thomas Kelly*

There are a number of us who creep
    Into the world to eat and sleep;
And know no reason why we're born,
    But only to consume the corn,
Devour the cattle, flesh and fish,
    And leave behind an empty dish.
And if our tombstone, when we die,
    Be not taught to flatter and to lie,
There's nothing better can be said
    Than that he's eaten up all his bread,
Drunk up his drink, and gone to bed.—*Isaac Watts*

Gadara, AD 31

Rabbi, begone! Thy powers
Bring loss to us and ours.
Our ways are not as Thine.
Thou lovest men, we—swine.
  Oh, get You hence, Omnipotence,
  And take this fool of Thine!
  His soul? What care we for his soul?
  What good to us that Thou hast made him whole,
  Since we have lost our swine?
And Christ went sadly.
He had wrought for them a sign
Of Love, and Hope, and Tenderness divine;
They wanted—swine.
  Christ stands without your door and gently knocks;
  But if your gold, or swine, the entrance blocks,
  He forces no man's hold—He will depart,
  And leave you to the treasures of your heart.
No cumbered chamber will the Master share,
But one swept bare
By cleansing fires, then plenished fresh and fair
With meekness, and humility, and prayer.
  There will He come, yet, coming, even there
  He stands and waits, and will no entrance win
  Until the latch be lifted from within.—*John Oxenham*

Unchanging

For feelings come and feelings go,
And feelings are deceiving:
My warrant is the Word of God,
Naught else is worth believing.
    Though all my heart should feel condemned
    For want of some sweet token,
    There is One greater than my heart,
    Whose Word cannot be broken.
I'll trust in God's unchanging Word
Till soul and body sever:
For though all things shall pass away,
His Word shall stand forever.—*Martin Luther*

I feel sorry for the guys
Who criticize and minimize
The other guys
Whose enterprise
Has made them rise
Above the guys
Who criticize and minimize.—*James Cole*

Mr. Tattat
You must not pat
Your arguments flat
On the crown of another man's hat.—*C.H. Spurgeon*

207

God Moves in a Mysterious Way

God moves in a mysterious way
    His wonders to perform;
He plants His footsteps in the sea,
    And rides upon the storm.
Deep in unfathomable mines
    Of never-failing skill
He treasures up His bright designs,
    And works His sovereign will.
Ye fearful saints, fresh courage take,
    The clouds ye so much dread
Are big with mercy, and shall break
    In blessing on your head.
Judge not the Lord by feeble sense
    But trust Him for His grace:
Behind a frowning providence
    He hides a smiling face.
His purposes will ripen fast,
    Unfolding every hour;
The bud may have a bitter taste
    But sweet will be the flower.
Blind unbelief is sure to err
    And scan His work in vain;
God is His own interpreter
    And He will make it plain.—*William Cowper*

Theology

There is a heaven, forever, day by day
The upward longing of my soul doth tell me so.
There is a hell, I'm quite as sure; for pray
If there were not, where would my neighbors go?
                              —*Paul Laurence Dunbar*

We are the Chosen Few,
All others will be damned;
There is no place up here for you,
We can't have heaven crammed.—*Anonymous*

Arabian Proverb:

He who knows not, and knows not that he knows not,
    he is a fool. Shun him.
He who knows not, and knows that he knows not,
    he is simple. Teach him.
He who knows and knows not that he knows,
    he is asleep. Wake him.
He who knows and knows that he knows,
    he is wise. Follow him.

The Present Crisis

Truth forever on the scaffold,
Wrong forever on the throne—
Yet that scaffold sways the future,
And, behind the dim unknown,
Standeth God within the shadow,
Keeping watch above His own.—*James R. Lowell*

209

Prayer: Results

Jacob prayed: the angel blessed him, Esau's revenge changed to fraternal love.

Joseph prayed: he was delivered from the pit to the prison to the palace of the Pharaoh.

Moses prayed; Miriam's life was spared; Amalek discomfited, Israel triumphed.

Joshua prayed: the sun stood still, victory was gained.

Esther prayed: Mordecai exalted, hateful Haman hanged.

David prayed: the traitor Ahithophel hanged himself.

Hannah prayed; she became the mother of Samuel.

Asa prayed: Judah gained a glorious victory.

Jehoshaphat prayed: God turned away His anger and smiled.

Elijah prayed: drought scorched, fire fell, rain descended and the earth was renewed.

Elisha prayed; the waters of Jordan divided, a child was restored to life.

Isaiah prayed: thousands of enemy Assyrian soldiers died.

Hezekiah prayed: the sun dial was turned back, his life was prolonged for 15 years.

Nehemiah prayed: the king's heart was softened in a moment.

The disciples prayed: the Holy Spirit came, the sick were healed.

The church prayed: Peter was delivered from prison.

Paul and Silas prayed: the prison shook, doors opened, fetters fell.

PASTOR'S PAL

Power: Environment

We pray for patience, and God sends those who tax us to the utmost, for "tribulation worketh patience." We pray for submission, and God sends suffering, for we learn obedience by the things we suffer. We pray for unselfishness, and God gives opportunities to sacrifice ourselves by thinking on the "things of others."

We pray for victory, and the things of the world sweep down upon us like a storm of temptation, for "this is the victory that overcometh the world, even our faith." We pray for humility and strength, and some messenger of Satan torments us until we lie in the dust, crying to God for its removal. We pray for union with Jesus, and God severs natural ties and lets our best friends misunderstand or become indifferent to us.

We pray for more love, and God sends peculiar suffering and puts us with apparently unlovely persons, letting them say things to rasp the nerves, lacerate the heart and sting the conscience; for love suffers long and is kind; love is not impolite; love is not provoked; love bears; love believes, hopes and endures; love never fails.

We ask to follow Jesus, and He separates us from home and kindred, for He Himself said, "Whosoever he be of you that forsaketh not all that he hath, he cannot be My disciple." We pray for the Lamb of life and are given a portion of lowly service, or we are injured and must seek no redress; for He was led as a Lamb to the slaughter and opened not His mouth.

We pray for gentleness, and there comes a perfect storm of temptation to yield to harshness and irritability. We pray for quietness, and everything within and around is confusion, that we may learn when He giveth quietness no one can make trouble.

—Hulda Stumpf

We see then that God does not always answer when, where and in the way that we may desire, but rather He "moves in a mysterious way His wonders to perform." And then, it does not really matter, for we have this assurance—He is able to do far more abundantly above all that we ask or think!

Preachers in Politics

Ministers actively engaged in politics claim they desire to help their people. This sounds altruistic, noble. But the help which they offer is primarily materialistic. Their talk about the "whole man"—preaching a holistic gospel—frequently turns out to be a religious-flavored emphasis on the physical and material things of life. They fail to realize that man is better off as a whole being only when the spiritual things of life are put first. This is why Christ said, "But seek first the kingdom of God and His righteousness, and all these things shall be added to you" (Matt. 6:33). And again, "For what will it profit a man if he gains the whole world, and loses his own soul?" (Mark 8:36).

In other words, the highest good the preacher can do is help win people to a saving knowledge of Jesus Christ, encourage Christians to set their affections on things above—i.e., their treasures in heaven—and their thoughts on the life hereafter. We are to stress clean living in a dirty age, the separated life, holiness, prayerfulness and the study of the Word of God. Without these things there can be no real permanent good.

We are hard-pressed for any New Testament evidence to support the contention that Christian ministers should be actively engaged in politics. Zealots wanted the Lord Jesus to "run for office," proclaim Himself king and overthrow the Roman oppressor. But He refused, and the carnal-minded, the cross materialists of His day, were greatly disappointed by the Lord's refusal to become politically involved. Even so, at His trial His enemies hurled at him charges of sedition and conspiracy against Caesar.

But Christ still refused to become involved. And so did Peter, and James, and John. And so did Paul, who, according to the book of Acts, was accused of being a bad citizen and starting riots, turning the world upside down and preaching another king—not Caesar, but the resurrected Jesus Christ!

It appears that politics can be a dirty game, often full of fraud, guile, hypocrisy and deceit. If there is any one person who ought to be free of these, it is the preacher. He is to sit in judgment upon an immoral society and be above the dirt, hypocrisy, respect of persons, corruption and fraud of the political arena. The failure to maintain this freedom is failure to be useful, either to God or man. How can any preacher perform in these two roles—preacher and politician—without compromise?

Can he participate in the many worldly affairs, the dances, cocktail parties, etc.? Does he attempt to serve two masters? Can we really see involvement in politics as an extension of ministry? One gets the feeling that the church is only being used by the politicians. Many Black pastors, worried about a resurgence of racial violence, are working to channel ghetto frustrations into more power at the polls—and to revive their own influence. Churches have been political springboards for some Black ministers. Only by subterfuge can churches make noncorporate donations to political campaigns. In their zeal to see one of their own elected, Black Baptists have hastened their own spiritual decline. Politics cannot solve all the problems of society because not all our problems are political. The preacher turned politician contradicts his calling, no longer willing to fight only with faith and the Bible, but turning spiritual power into worldly power play.

At that point he saddles the church with a role for which it is not equipped. Politics is then made our new god; politics is idolized. Our motto becomes, "Seek ye first the political kingdom, and . . ." Certainly there is the danger of mixing Biblical and political issues together in one lump. Political change, the establishment of good laws, etc., is no substitute for heart change. Fighting moral issues with political muscle is a high-risk venture. We must not pin our hopes on the fortunes of the erratic political process. Political majority may not be God's will.

Preachers who enter politics cause the local church to suffer. Pastoring a church is no easy task and becoming increasingly more difficult. It is a twenty-four-hour-a-day job. Holding a political office is a second job. The world seeks to win most of the preacher's time; it wants to be first in his heart and affection. The result? Less and less time is spent in prayer, Bible study and the preparation of sermons.

And the church suffers. Preachers should not enter politics because it is a violation of Baptist polity concerning the separation of church and state. Preachers should not enter politics because it is a violation of their calling. We are called to give ourselves continually to prayer and to the ministry of the Word of God (Acts 6:4).

We are called to open the eyes of the lost, to turn them from darkness to light and from the power of Satan to God, that they may receive forgiveness of sins and an inheritance among those who are sanctified in Christ. We are called to preach the gospel: Christ crucified, buried and risen.

We are called to preach the Word!

> Be ready in season and out of season. Convince, rebuke, exhort, with all longsuffering and teaching. For the time will come when they will not endure sound doctrine, but according to their own desires, because they have itching ears, they will heap up for themselves teachers; and they will turn their ears away from the truth, and be turned aside to fables. But you be watchful in all things, endure afflictions, do the work of an evangelist, fulfill your ministry. (2 Tim. 4:2–5)

The man called into the ministry ought to realize that he has been highly favored and blessed of God. For no man takes this honor to himself; but he is called by God, just as Aaron was (Heb. 5:4). Amen!

Preaching: Things to Look For

1. Christ-centeredness
2. Biblical: Scriptural undergirding
3. Text
4. Interpretation
5. Preparation and knowledge of material
6. Posture/Poise
7. Gestures
8. Diction, Enunciation
9. Outline: Introduction, Body, Conclusion
10. Type of Sermon:
    a. Expository
    b. Textual
    c. Topical
11. Method of Delivery
    a. Read
    b. Extempore
    c. Memowrite: write out and deliver from memory
12. Eye-to-eye contact
13. Use of Emphasis:
    a. Pause
    b. Pitch
    c. Progress (speaking rapidly or slowly)
    d. Punch (speaking loudly or softly)

14. Grammar
15. Illustrations
16. Practical application
17. Sincerity

Remembrances

Psalm 103:2: "Bless the Lord, O my soul, and forget none of His benefits." I can still remember the times when I had:

No ark of safety in the time of flood
No city of refuge to flee to
No manna from heaven to feed upon
No Friend to stick closer than a brother
No peace in the valley
No beauty to behold
No deliverer from Egypt
No desire to go on living
No shield to quench Satan's fiery darts
No escape in the night
No High Tower to run into
No angel to shake my dungeon, break my shackles or cool my fiery furnace
No Shield or Buckler to protect me
No Captain to lead me in victory
No Balm in Gilead, no Physician to heal me
No heaven in my view
No Bright Morning Star in my sky
No Comforter to strengthen me
No Spirit to fill me

No Good Shepherd to call me by my name
No oasis in the desert
No well of water to quench my thirst
No Promised Land in my sight
No love in my heart
No bright mansion above
No song in my mouth
No melody in my soul
No praise upon my lips
No eternity on my mind
No lawyer to plead my case
No crown on my head
No spring in my steps
No robe for my back
No God in my thoughts
No hope for tomorrow
No help for today
No joy in my spirit
No blood to cleanse away my sins!

But now I can thank God for all His blessings and benefits!
For the Lord Jesus Christ shed His blood for my sins and bought
me out of the slave market. And from Him all blessings flow.

Salvation

Past	Present	Future
Greek: Rom. 8:24; Eph. 2:5, 8 2 Tim. 1:9	Greek: 1 Cor. 1:18; 2 Cor 2:15 1 Cor. 15:2	Greek: Rom. 10:9
I was saved, or I have been saved	I am being saved	I shall be saved Rom 13:11
Christ crucified	Christ risen	Christ coming back
Justification Rom. 5:1	Sanctification (also past, present and future)	Glorification, Rom. 8:30; note past tense
Penalty of sin Rom. 6:23	Power of sin Rom. 6:12–14	Presence of sin
Spirit	Soul	Body: Phil. 3:21; 1 John 3:2; 1 Thess. 4:17; 1 Cor. 15:51ff.
Look back	Look up	Look forward
Possess	Experience	Anticipate

Selah

The word *selah* is used more than seventy times in the Psalms and is found three times in Habakkuk. It first occurs in Psalm 3:2 and is last used in Habakkuk 3:13. *Selah* comes from a verb meaning "to lift up, exalt." In relation to music it indicates a pause, as when the musician lifts his hands from the instrument. As a word used in the psalms that were sung, *selah* indicates some kind of change was to be made in the music.

However its meaning is uncertain. Opinions vary as to the exact nature of the word, but it seems to be a technical term for the benefit of the musical director and the instrumentalists. Perhaps it was a time for the singers to pause and meditate upon the words they had been singing. Or maybe it indicated an increase in volume.

Research suggests the word should not be taken necessarily as a part of the original text inspired by God. For this reason some Bible versions omit it altogether or place it in parentheses, signifying it should not be read. Ordinarily, unless our purpose is to teach, we do not read *selah*. To read a Hebrew word and not tell the meaning of it does not edify. If teaching, read it and explain it. If reading the psalm for public hearing, do ***not*** read *selah*. Just as we do not read the headings found in many of the psalms, so the word *selah* ought not be read aloud in the public assembly.

Seven Last Words

First Word: Luke 23:34
Second Word: Luke 23:43
Third Word: John 19:26–27
Fourth Word: Matthew 27:46
Fifth Word: John 19:28
Sixth Word: John 19:30
Seventh Word: Luke 23:46

Presented here are seed thoughts, suggestions for preaching during this glorious holy week. No attempt is made to provide exhaustive material, nor should the pastor try to use all of these ideas in any one given message.

No pain, no palm; No thorn, no throne:
No gall, no glory; No cross, no crown. —William Penn

FIRST WORD

Then Jesus said, "Father, forgive them, for they do not know what they do." (Luke 23: 34)

1. A contemporary model of a forgiving heart.
2. Note, there is absolutely no bitterness expressed here,

only the words of a magnanimous spirit.

3. Forgive them. Who? Jews and Gentiles. Are we included for our part in His crucifixion? Negro spiritual: "Were You There . . . ?"

4. Believers: Forgiveness (Eph. 4:32)—to be gracious.

5. Examples of Forgiveness:
   a. Jacob and Esau (Gen. 33:4)
   b. Joseph and his brothers (Gen. 45:15, 50:15–21)
   c. Moses and his sister, Miriam (Num. 12:13)
   d. David and Absalom (2 Sam. 14:21–33)
   e. Stephen (Acts 7:59–60)

6. Forgiveness is a two-way street: He offered; have we received?

7. Forgiveness does not necessarily mean there are no scars resulting from past sins.

8. He is a Savior who is always willing to forgive (1 John 1:9).

9. Hymn: "If I Have Wounded Any Soul Today"

10. Do you pray for your enemies? (Rom. 12:19–20; Matt. 6:14)

11. Are there varying degrees of responsibility for sin? (Luke 12:48)

12. Ignorance is no excuse; forgiveness is still needed.

13. Sins of ignorance (Lev. 5:15; Num. 15:24–26).

14. More on ignorance (Acts 3:13–18; 1 Cor. 2:6–8).

15. Ignorantly in unbelief (1 Tim. 1:13).

SECOND WORD

And Jesus said to him, "Assuredly, I say to you, today you will be with Me in Paradise." (Luke 23:43)

1. Today: There is no intervening "soul-sleep." The Watchtower Society's rendering, *"Truly, I tell you today, you will be with me in Paradise"* (New World Translation), is simply untenable. The word "today" goes with the words, "you will be with Me." There is no in-between place (2 Cor. 5:6–8; Phil. 1:21–23; 1 Thess. 5:10).

2. Christ caused a split. Two robbers (a better rendering than *thieves*), partners in crime (Matt. 10:35; Luke 17:34–36), would soon be separated.

3. "And He made His grave with the wicked . . . and He was numbered with the transgressors" (Isa. 53:9, 12).

4. Hymn: "There Is a Fountain Filled with Blood"

5. Grace: The robber had been a robber for a long time, but there on the cross he had nothing—no works, no baptism, nothing in his hands but nails.

6. Paradise (Luke 16:23ff.; 2 Cor. 12:4; Rev. 2:7): To be with Him is Paradise!

7. The joy of being with Him (John 1:43, 12:26, 17:24; 1 Thess. 4:17; Phil. 1:23).

8. The solemn promise of salvation.

THIRD WORD

John 19:26–27: "Woman, behold your son! . . . Behold your mother!" (John 19:26–27)

1. To address Mary as "woman" perhaps sounds harsh to our ears today, but it was a title of courtesy and respect in the Orient. One thing is sure; she is not the Queen of Heaven, or the Mother of God, or Co-Redemptrix. Blessed of women, yes; but still a sinner who needed a Savior (Luke 1:47).

2. Imagine how Mary felt! How could this happen to her firstborn? (Luke 2:7). But as Simeon predicted, her soul was to be pierced through also (Luke 2:35).

3. See our Lord's compassionate thoughtfulness. In the midst of excruciating pain, in His very hour of death, His one earthly concern is for Mary's welfare.

4. But why John? Since there is no mention of Joseph, it is assumed he was dead. None of the half-brothers of our Lord believed in Him at that time (John 7:5). But John was the nearest believing male relative and evidently the only disciple who appeared at the cross.

5. Hymn: "He Cares, O Yes, He Cares!"

6. Intimacy with John (Mark 3:17, 9:38, 10:35ff.; Luke 9:54).

FOURTH WORD

My God, My God, why have You forsaken Me? (Mark 15:34).

1. A holy God hates sin but loves the sinner. Sinless Christ became sin in order to pay sin's penalty (2 Cor. 5:21).

2. He was made a curse (Gal. 3:13), and God turned com-

pletely away from Him.

3. Note He cried, "My God" and not "My Father!"

4. Sin separates, causes forsakenness, abandonment (Isa. 59:2).

5. Psalm 22:1: "My God, My God, why have You forsaken Me? Why are You so far from helping Me, and from the words of My groaning?"

6. Christ was deserted that we might be drawn nigh to God.

7. Separation from God is death; it is hell.

8. Jesus Christ is God who became a Man. As a Man He has a God. The words spoken in John 20:17, after the resurrection ("I am ascending to My Father and your Father, and to My God and your God") basically show a difference between our Lord's relationship to God and the relationship of the disciples to God.

9. The forsakenness or tasting of God's wrath by Christ was endured on the cross, not after His death. At the point of death our Lord committed His spirit into the hands of the Father (Luke 23:46).

10. He promised never to leave us alone (Heb. 13:5; Matt. 28:20): Hymn: "Never Alone."

FIFTH WORD

I thirst. (John 19:28)

1. The Greek word, *dipso*, gives us *dipsomaniac*, one with an insatiable, periodic craving for alcoholic beverages.

2. *Dipso* may refer to a compelling desire to do something or possess something. It is used of righteousness and a thirsting after God (Matt. 5:6; Ps. 42:2, 63:1, 143:6).
3. Concerning suffering from thirst: Matt. 25:35, 37, 42, 44; John 4:15; Rom. 12:20; 1 Cor. 4:11; (noun: 2 Cor. 11:27).
4. Figure of speech: John 4:13–14, 6:35, 7:37; Rev. 7:16, 21:6, 22:17. To thirst here is to painfully feel the want of, or eagerly long for, those things by which the soul is refreshed, supported, strengthened (Thayer).
5. Imagine the Creator of oceans, rivers, streams, the Giver of rain in due season (Lev. 26:4)—crying out, "I thirst!"
6. The Rock from which water flows, the Quencher of Thirst, cries, "I thirst" (Num. 20:8; Neh. 9:15, 20; 1 Cor. 10:4).
7. Man's need for water is greater than his need for food.
8. Ps. 69:21: "And in my thirst they gave me vinegar to drink."
9. Hymn:
   I heard the voice of Jesus say:
      "Behold, I freely give
   The living water; thirsty one,
      Stoop down, and drink, and live."
   I came to Jesus, and I drank
      Of that life-giving stream:
   My thirst was quenched, my soul revived,
      And now I live in Him.—H. Bonar

SIXTH WORD

It is finished! (John 19:30)

1. Here is a shout of victory! And our Lord always leads us in triumph (2 Cor. 2:14).
2. The joy of completing your task (Heb. 12:2).
3. This is one word in the original language—*tetelestai*: It has been completed or accomplished (John 19:28). Use of the perfect tense indicates that what was started at some time in the past, has right-now, present results. Use of the passive voice indicates action effected from the outside. Because of the crucifixion, His work stands in a completed condition.
4. A Finished Work! (John 4:34, 17:4)
5. See the assurance of perseverance. Here is a fulfilled purpose, ordained from the beginning of the world.
6. Hymn: "Jesus Paid It All"
7. *Lifted up was He to die, "It is finished," was His cry:*
   Now in heav'n exalted high: Hallelujah! What a Savior!
   —Philip P. Bliss

8. *Calv'ry's mournful mountain climb:*
   There, adoring at His feet,
   Mark that miracle of time.
   God's own sacrifice complete:
   "It is finished!" hear the cry:
   Learn of Jesus Christ to die.
   —James Montgomery

SEVENTH WORD

Father, into Your hands I commend My spirit. (Luke 23:46)

1. Psalm 31:5: "Into Your hand I commend my spirit; You have redeemed me, O Lord God of truth."
2. Christ (Luke 23:46), centurion (Luke 23:47; Mark 15:39), crowd (Luke 23:48), companion (Luke 23:49).
3. The hands of God (Exod. 15:6; Josh. 4:24; Ezra 7:9; Neh. 2:8; Job 2:10, KJV; Ps. 16:1, 17:7; Isa. 40:12, 41:10, 59:1; Dan. 5:23; Amos 9:2; John 10:29).
4. The voluntary nature of His death (John 10:18)
5. "To commend" is to entrust for safekeeping, to deposit (Acts 14:23, 20:32). In Psalm 31:5 "to commit" is to charge, trust. See Numbers 4:16 where the word is rendered *oversight*; Jeremiah 36:20, *stored, laid up* and Jeremiah 37:21, *commit*.
6. Famous last words: Reactions in a dying hour. See Brewer's *Dictionary of Phrase and Fable*.
7. Triumphant declaration of a confident faith.
8. Hymns: "Hold to God's Unchanging Hand"; "In the Hollow of His Hand."

Sevens

SEVEN-FOLD ABILITY OF GOD

1. He is able to deliver (Dan. 3:17; cf. 6:20).
2. He is able to provide for good works (2 Cor. 9:8).
3. He is able to do more than we may ask or think (Eph. 3:20).
4. He is able to keep His promises (Rom. 4:21).
5. He is able to keep our deposit (2 Tim. 1:12).
6. He is able to save thoroughly and completely (Heb. 7:25).
7. He is able to keep us from fatally, finally falling (Jude 24).

SEVEN INDISPENSABLES

1. Without Me you can do nothing (John 15:5).
2. Without love I am nothing (1 Cor. 13:2).
3. Without shedding of blood there is no remission (sending away, forgiveness) of sin (Heb. 9:22).
4. Without faith it is impossible to please God (Heb. 11:6).
5. Without chastisement you are not sons (Heb. 12:8).
6. Without holiness no man shall see the Lord (Heb. 12:14).
7. Without works faith is dead (James 2:26).

SEVEN THINGS GOD HAS DONE WITH OUR SINS

1. Removed our sins as far as the east is from the west, out of reach (Ps. 103:12)
2. Cast all our sins behind His back, out of the way (Isa. 38:17)
3. Blotted them out, to be remembered no more, out of view (Isa. 43:25)
4. Swept away like a thick cloud, out of existence (Isa. 44:22)
5. Cast our sins into the depths of the sea, out of sight (Mic. 7:19)
6. Has forgiven all our trespasses, out of danger (Col. 2:13)
7. Sins and iniquities remembered no more, out of mind (Heb. 10:17)

Stewardship

HOW TO GIVE

I. We Are to Give Without:

Show: Matthew 6:1–4: The motive behind our giving is not a desire to be seen of men. Eye-service displeases the Lord (Eph. 6:6; Col. 3:22).

Acts 5:1–11: This husband-and-wife team had every right to do as they pleased with their possessions. There was no need to lie to the Holy Spirit, who is God. But the desire to make a big show and impress others with their supposed generosity was one of the motives that led them to tell a lie and pay for it with their lives.

Self: Acts 20:35: There is no record in the Gospels of Christ having said these exact words, but it is a fact that the greater blessing lies in the habit of continuously giving rather than in taking or receiving.

Sorrow: 2 Corinthians 9:6–7: We are not to give grudgingly or, literally, from grief. We should not be sorry the money slipped out of our hands; or feel that our arms were twisted to give, made to give, compelled or afraid of the consequences of not giving. God loves a cheerful (the word *hilarious* is derived from the original) giver—a light-hearted, joyous, happy giver! (Prov. 22:9).

Stealing: Malachi 3:8–9: Tithing is mentioned before the giving of the Law at Mount Sinai (Gen. 14:20, 28:22), but it became a requirement under the Law system (Lev. 27:30; Num. 18:21–24; Deut. 14:22–29). So those Jews who failed to obey this law were accused of robbing or short-changing God. New Testament Christians recognize also that Christ is Lord over all of our possessions. Shall we who are under grace in the church age give less than did the Jews under the Law system?

Stinginess: Proverbs 11:25: In the Old Testament the idiom "to be fat" means to be enriched, made prosperous, well-nourished, productive. So the verse teaches: Don't be stingy, or you'll be a skinny, string-bean, sad-sack sight of a saint. A soul of blessing is one from whom blessings go out to others. When you do not give out, you do not take in. Thus the text says, "Stingy out, stingy in." But "he who waters will also be watered himself" or "fat out, fat in." The blessing you give out comes back to you.

II. We Are to Give With:

Sacrifice: 2 Sam. 24:24: These are beautiful words: "Neither will I offer burnt offerings to the Lord my God with that which costs me nothing." David came to set up an altar unto the Lord in the threshing floor of a man named Araunah, the Jebusite, and offered to pay for the threshing floor and the oxen. But Araunah offered it free of charge. David refused, then bought it. You see, some people have an easy, self-indulgent faith. They give God their left-overs, discards, superfluous, out-of-date, no-longer-wanted, out-of-style, junk. There is no sense of sacrifice involved in their hearts at all. It is like offering to God something I intended to throw out on the junk pile anyway but thought, "Oh, God, would You like to have this?" (1 Sam. 1:28; Phil. 4:18; Eph. 5:2). Incidentally, the word translated "spoils" in Hebrews 7:4 is literally "top of the heap," or as we would say, "the cream of the crop." There is to be no scraping of the bottom of the barrel here.

Simplicity: Romans 12:8: The word rendered "simplicity" or "liberality" means, literally, "without folds, without wrinkles." In Ephesians 6:5 (KJV) and Colossians 3:22 (KJV), it is translated as "single," thus free from duplicity, pretense, dissimulation; nothing complicated or confused. Take two sheets of clear paper; crumple one and compare it with the clear sheet. What are some of the folds, creases or wrinkles in our giving?

Systematically: 1 Corinthians 16:2: Definiteness is the key. *A definite time*: upon the first day of the week. *A definite person*: Let every one of you (no unbelievers). *A definite act*: lay by him in store. *A definite proportion*: As God has prospered you. We cannot come empty-handed (Exod. 23:15, 34:19–20): Bring something to worship in your heart, hands, head, lips (Hosea 14:2). *A definite reason*: that there be no gatherings when I come.

Spirituality: Galatians 6:7–9: Don't fool yourself: nobody derides, mocks, sneers or turns his nose up at God with impunity. When we give money in ways well-pleasing to the Lord: (1) others are blessed; (2) by means of their thanksgiving, God is blessed or praised; (3) we who give are blessed (Prov. 11:24). 2 Corinthians 8:12: The Lord looks at the spirit in which the giving is done, so that if you are eager to give, what you give will be accepted and you need not worry about what you don't possess or how much you do not have that you can give. The "bottom line" of stewardship is: God so loved that He gave! (2 Cor. 8:9; John 3:16).

What shall your epitaph read?
Here lies a miser who lived for himself
And cared nothing but gathering pelf.
Now, where is he, or how does he fare?
Nobody knows, and no one doth care.

Stewardship:
Sermon Texts

Deut. 16:17: As Able, As Blessed, As Unto the Lord
Ps. 24:1: It's His Anyhow!
Ps. 103:1–2: Soul Blessing
Ps. 116:12–14: How to Repay God
Prov. 3:9: Give of Your Best
Prov. 13:7 (11:24): A Poor Rich Man
Matt. 6:19–21: Treasures in Heaven
Matt. 6:33: First Things First
Mark 4:24–25: Use or Lose
Mark 8:36: Profit and Loss Statement
Luke 12:15: Possessions that Possess
1 Cor. 4:2: Faithful Stewards
1 Tim. 6:17–19: An Eternally Safe Investment

A Toast

Our prayer for you is that you may be as:

Worshipful as Abel
Capable as Abigail
A friend of God as was Abraham
Devout as Anna
Steadfast as Caleb
Brave as Daniel
Zealous for God like David
Patriotic as Deborah
Benevolent as Dorcas
A rescuer like Ebed-Melech
Fiery as Elijah
Surrendered as Elisha
Walk with God as did Enoch
Helpful as Epaphroditus
Willing to sacrifice as was Esther
Have visions like Ezekiel
Bold as Gideon
Grateful as Hannah
Patient as Job
Loving as John
Loyal as Jonathan

With the integrity of Joseph
Courageous as Joshua
Hospitable as Lydia
Live as long as Methuselah
Meek as Moses
Alert as Nehemiah
Have faith like Noah
Prayerful as Paul
Leader like Peter
Useful as Priscilla
Observant as the Queen of Sheba
Constant as Ruth
Dedicated as Samuel
Strong as Samson
Devoted as Simeon
Wise as Solomon
Spirit-filled as Stephen

Take all their good points, roll them together and get a glimpse of the beauty of the character of the Lord Jesus. In short, my prayer for you is that you may continue to become more like Him who loved us and gave Himself for us.

Trustees

Trustees are officers required by state laws. They are not, however, scriptural officers, and care should be taken to maintain scriptural leadership in the church. They should not be allowed to handle money *and* also determine administrative policies. Their responsibility is to be good stewards of the church property entrusted to their care. Trustees should be elected annually. Some assemblies have tenure restrictions, but usually in our churches there is a shortage of qualified personnel for this office, so that tenure may be impractical.

Use of women trustees does not violate the scriptures prohibiting women usurping authority over men in the church (1 Tim. 2:12). It is not, however, recommended that a woman be made the chairman of the Trustee Board. Trustees should be knowledgeable and successful managers of their own property or that of the organization which employs them. Combined with a deep sense of spiritual commitment, trustees should use their expertise or seek that of people who have the skill and experience to do a job for the church. The pastor should be involved as the adviser and be an administrative officer with the trustees; he may be able to provide expert guidance and support because of his contacts. Trustees are not given authority to restrict the pastor's use of church property for religious services or other proper meetings. They should not be permitted to grant the use of the church to other persons or groups without the knowledge and consent of the pastor.

Women Preachers/Pastors

1. There were no women in the priesthood of Israel (Exod. 28:1, 40:15; Lev. 21; Heb. 5:1–4).
2. The Lord Jesus called no women into the apostleship (Matt. 10:2–5).
3. The fact that women carried the message of Christ's resurrection was an honor, but it has nothing to do with holding positions of authority over men. The church was not established until the Day of Pentecost. Whereas the daughters of Philip prophesied, there is no record they did so while holding a position of authority over men in the church. Priscilla also taught Apollos in private.
4. 1 Corinthians 14:4 altogether forbids women to be tongues speakers; 1 Corinthians 14 discourages gibberish.
5. No mention of women pastors in the church.
6. Old Testament Jewish prophetesses and women who will prophesy during the Tribulation (Acts 2:17; Joel 2:28–29), have nothing to do with the church age, coming centuries after Deborah's ministry. Joel's prophecy remains to be fulfilled; no celestial phenomena occurred at Pentecost.
7. Galatians 3:28 deals with salvation and standing, not with function, or division of labor or holding office in the church. Conversion did not erase distinctions between male and female; slaves were not set free. Spiritual privilege is not the same as spiritual activity.

8. 1 Timothy 2:12 is very explicit: *The woman is not to hold office over the man in the church.* She is not to exercise authority over the man in doctrinal or disciplinary matters. The word *didaskein* is not in the aorist tense, which signifies "not to teach at any time," but is the present infinitive, meaning "to be a teacher"—holding the position of teacher over men in the church.

9. Paul based his argument upon priority in creation, not merely Jewish custom. God made man the head of the woman (Gen. 3:16; 1 Cor. 11:3).

10. The fact of Eve's deception, the readiness with which she was deceived (completely, thoroughly), ill-fits her for leadership in matters of church doctrine and discipline (Gen. 3:13). Adam deliberately sinned; Eve was fooled.

11. It is manifestly impossible for a woman to qualify as *the husband of one wife*, one of the requirements to be a bishop (a title for pastor, it means *overseer*: 1 Tim. 3:1–2).

12. There are psychological, physiological, functional differences—not considered superior or inferior—between men and women. Attempts to obliterate these differences (Deut. 22:5) are sinful, wicked perversions of God's will.

13. Psalm 68:11 (NASB): The women who proclaim the good tidings are a great host; they sing songs announcing military victories. It has nothing to do with their holding positions of authority over men in the church.

Conclusion: Do not let the negative weight you give to any one of these arguments undermine the cumulative effect.